Birds of Myanmar

by

Kyaw Nyunt Lwin
Khin Ma Ma Thwin

Illustrated by

Aung Thant

SILKWORM BOOKS

ISBN 974-9575-68-7

First published in 2003 by
Swiftwinds, Yangon

This edition is published in 2005 by
Silkworm Books
6 Sukkasem Road, Chiang Mai 50200, Thailand
E-mail: silkworm@silkwormbooks.info
Website: www.silkwormbooks.info

Set in 8 pt. Stone Serif

Printed by O. S. Printing House, Bangkok

5 4 3 2 1

CONTENTS

INTRODUCTION

The aim of this book is to fill the literary gap in Myanmar about its birdlife, and provide updated information in order to create an interest in the study of birds and their conservation.

The birds of Myanmar were the subject of a comprehensive book authored by Bertram E. Smythies who gathered information from his own observations during his tenure as a Forestry Officer in Myanmar in the 1930s and also from numerous published works that appeared during the preceeding century. The book *The Birds of Burma* was first published in Yangon in 1940; later editions, published outside Myanmar, were, however, not widely distributed domestically.

An attempt was made by the late U H. G. Hundley, retired Conservator of Forests and U Kyaw Nyunt Lwin in 1984 to bring out a book entitled *A Handbook of the Commoner Birds of Burma*. The text was written by U H. G. Hundley and the illustrations were organized by U Kyaw Nyunt Lwin. Regrettably the manuscript and the paintings were lost during negotiations for publication, and all the efforts to produce the book proved vain.

The present book is simple and non-technical, embracing commoner resident birds and winter visitors of Myanmar. The text compiled by U Kyaw Nyunt Lwin is meant to be as concise as possible. The illustrations, based on the specimens maintained at the Biodiversity Museum of Hlawga Wildlife Park and the plates of various bird books listed in the references, were drawn by U Aung Thant. Daw Khin Ma Ma Thwin who has a good deal of experience in the identification of birds from her field surveys, supervised and reviewed all the illustrations for accuracy and detail.

In the text, general notes on each family are given. This information, however, is not repeated in the species accounts. These start with the length (L) of the bird measured in inches from the tip of the bill to the tip of the tail with the neck outstretched. The appearance of the bird is described very briefly since this is apparent from the illustrations. It is followed by some information on habitat, behaviour, voice, breeding season and status. The distribution ranges given as N, E, W, SW etc. are shown on the map.

The birds are arranged as in *A Field Guide to the Birds of Thailand and South-East Asia* by Craig Robson, and the English names and the scientific names of the birds, as used in it, are also adopted in this book. The Myanmar names of the birds, as given in *The Birds of Burma* by Bertram E. Smythies, *Hnget-tha-bin* (Birds of Burma) by U Maung Maung Lay and the Myanmar-English Dictionary published by the Department of the Myanmar Language Commission, are duplicated here.

A check-list of all the bird species recorded in Myanmar up to the end of 2001 is also given in this book. The list, never published in any other bird book, was prepared by Daw Khin Ma Ma Thwin from the existing records and her own observations. The readers will also find useful the list of birds protected by law in Myanmar and the list of protected areas established in Myanmar up to the end of 2002.

In conclusion U Kyaw Nyunt Lwin would like to express his gratitude to Nagao Natural Environment Foundation (NEF) for their financial assistance in the production of this book; the Forest Resource Environment Development and Conservation Association (FREDA) and Dr. Kyaw Tint, Director-General (Retd) of Forest Department for their support and encouragement; U Khin Maung Zaw, Director of Nature and Wildlife Conservation Division of the Forest Department and

U Myint Sein, Park Warden of Hlawga Wildlife Park for allowing him and his team access to their records and specimens; U Aung Thant for his relentless work on all illustrations; and Swiftwinds Services Co., Ltd. for their cooperation in the publication of this onerous work.

We hope this book will bring about renewed interest in the birds and their conservation in Myanmar.

Kyaw Nyunt Lwin
Khin Ma Ma Thwin
November, 2003
Yangon, Myanmar

GEOGRAPHY

Myanmar, with a total land area of 261,228 sq.miles, lies between latitudes 10° and 29° N and longitudes 92° and 101°E. It is roughly diamond-shaped with the long "tail" of Tanintharyi extending southwards along the eastern shore of the Andaman Sea. Altitudes range from sea level to nearly 20,000 feet in the extreme north, with mountain ranges along western border with Bangladesh and India reaching 10,000 feet, and the Shan plateau in the east averaging 6,000–8,750 feet. The country is traversed by a number of great rivers flowing from north to south, of which the largest are the Ayeyarwady, with its western tributary, the Chindwin, and the Thanlwin which bisects in the east.

Apart from the mountains of the far north, the climate is generally tropical monsoonal with the heaviest rains during the south-west monsoon from May to October inclusive. Rainfall varies from over 250 inches in parts of Rakhine and Tanintharyi to less than 20 inches in the Dry Zone of the central lowlands, which is a rain-shadow area relative to the S W monsoon.

Approximately half the land area is covered with forests ranging from the subtropical and temperate evergreen forests of the northern mountains to the rain forests of Rakhine and Tanintharyi, and the mixed deciduous forest which is both the most extensive and the most economically important, producing teak and a number of other commercially valuable hardwoods. Other forest types are the tidal mangrove forests of Rakhine, the Ayeyarwady delta and Tanintharyi, the swamp forests, the dry forests of the central Dry Zone and the deciduous Dipterocarp forest or *Indaing*. Myanmar also possesses a great wealth and diversity of wetland ecosystems, ranging from permanent fresh water bodies of Inlay Lake, Indawgyi Lake, Mong Pai Lake, several major reservoirs and seasonally inundated floodplains of the main river systems during the monsoon to a coastline of about 1,425 miles with its several very large estuarine and delta systems and numerous offshore islands.

Zoogeographically, Myanmar forms a small part of the Oriental region and its favourable position gives it a very rich fauna and flora, both of which are Indian, Indochinese and Malaysian in composition.

BIRD TOPOGRAPHY

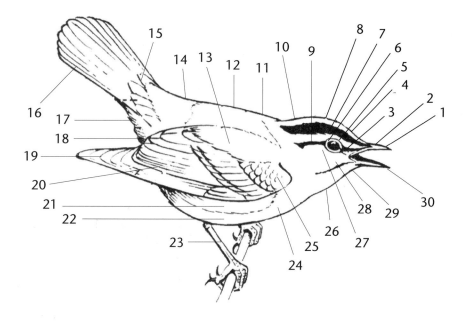

1. Upper mandible
2. Culmen
3. Lore
4. Forehead
5. Supercilium (eyebrow)
6. Eye-ring
7. Head-stripe
8. Crown
9. Eye-stripe (eye-line)
10. Nape
11. Mantle
12. Back
13. Scapulars
14. Rump
15. Upper tail coverts

16. Tail
17. Under tail coverts
18. Vent
19. Primaries
20. Secondaries
21. Flank
22. Belly
23. Tarsus
24. Breast
25. Wing coverts
26. Throat
27. Ear-coverts
28. Cheek
29. Chin
30. Lower mandible

MYANMAR
States and Divisions

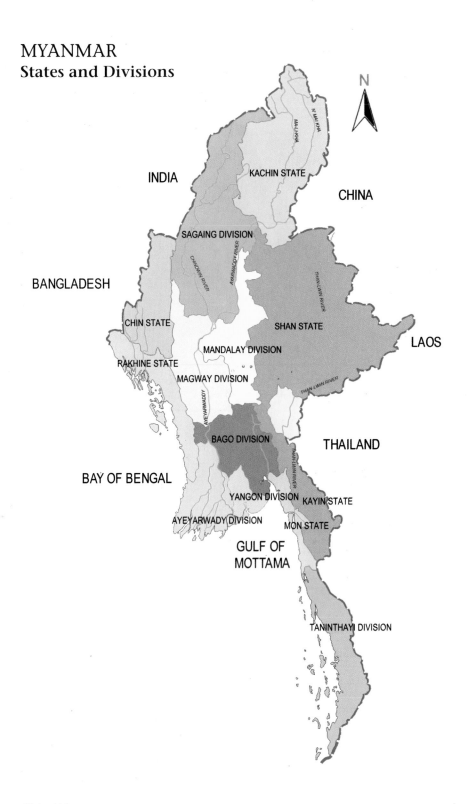

MYANMAR
Land elevations

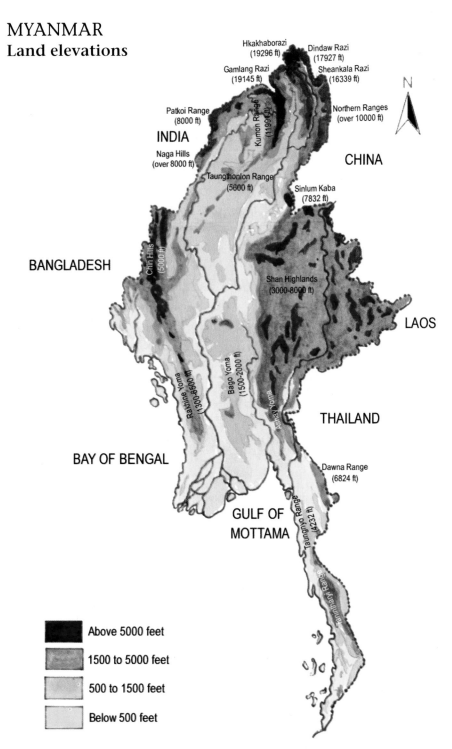

Hkakhaborazi
(19296 ft)

Dindaw Razi
(17927 ft)

Gamlang Razi
(19145 ft)

Sheankala Razi
(16339 ft)

Patkoi Range
(8000 ft)

Kumon Range
(11990 ft)

Northern Ranges
(over 10000 ft)

INDIA

Naga Hills
(over 8000 ft)

CHINA

Taungthonlon Range
(5600 ft)

Sinlum Kaba
(7832 ft)

Chin Hills
(5000 ft)

BANGLADESH

Shan Highlands
(3000-8000 ft)

LAOS

Rakhine Yoma
(1300-6500 ft)

Bago Yoma
(1500-2000 ft)

Arakan Yoma

THAILAND

BAY OF BENGAL

Dawna Range
(6824 ft)

GULF OF
MOTTAMA

Taungnyo Range
(4232 ft)

Tanintharyi Range

Above 5000 feet

1500 to 5000 feet

500 to 1500 feet

Below 500 feet

Source: Forest Department

x

Birds of Myanmar

MYANMAR
Distribution of dominant forest types

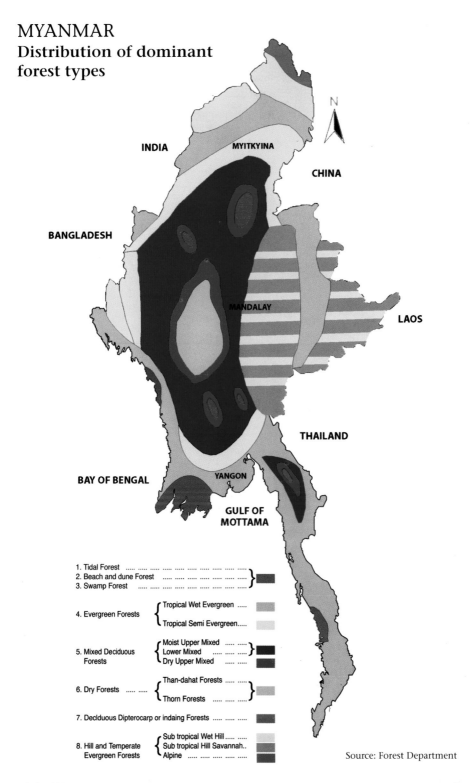

1. Tidal Forest   ....
2. Beach and dune Forest   ....
3. Swamp Forest   ....

4. Evergreen Forests
  Tropical Wet Evergreen .....
  Tropical Semi Evergreen.....

5. Mixed Deciduous Forests
  Moist Upper Mixed   ....
  Lower Mixed   ....
  Dry Upper Mixed   ....

6. Dry Forests   ....
  Than-dahat Forests ....
  Thorn Forests   ....

7. Deciduous Dipterocarp or indaing Forests   ....

8. Hill and Temperate Evergreen Forests
  Sub tropical Wet Hill ....
  Sub tropical Hill Savannah..
  Alpine   ....

Source: Forest Department

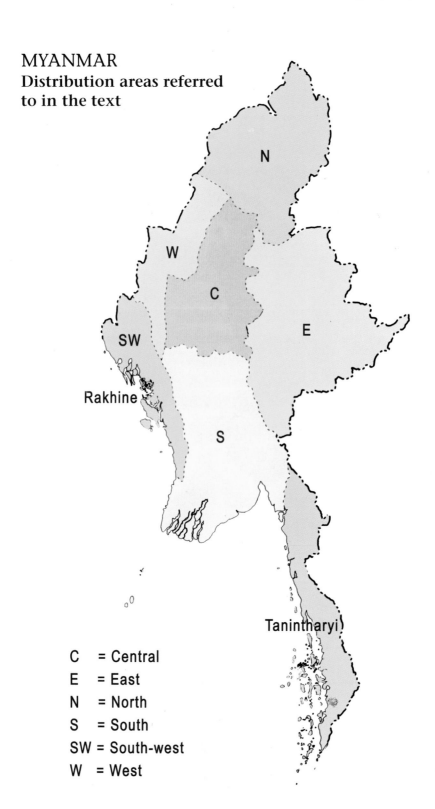

MYANMAR
Distribution areas referred to in the text

C = Central
E = East
N = North
S = South
SW = South-west
W = West

Birds of Myanmar

Species Accounts

QUAILS, PARTRIDGES, PHEASANTS Phasianidae

This family is represented in Myanmar by thirty-one species, of which twenty-nine are resident.

Members of this family are characterized by their plump bodies, strong unfeathered legs and strong bills. Sexes differ in most species, with the males more brightly coloured. They live on the ground, but perch and roost in trees. They run from danger rather than fly. They feed on seeds, berries, worms, insects etc. and lay their eggs on the ground, except for tragopans, which nest in trees. Most are gregarious.

Quails are small, round-bodied birds with very short tails; they live in grasslands and second growth. Partridges are larger birds with somewhat longer tails; they live in forests and second growth. Pheasants are larger birds with beautiful plumage; they are mainly found in forests; some species live in secondary growth and grassland.

1. CHINESE FRANCOLIN
Francolinus pintadeanus

L 13". A greyish bird, usually heard and not seen; male has white spots on mantle, neck, breast and upper belly; female has black bars on neck, breast and belly. Found in dry forests and second growth up to 5,000 feet, the Dry Zone of Myanmar being its stronghold. Solitary, sometimes paired. Often holds tail up when running. Feeds on grains, seeds and insects. Call: harsh, grating *do-be-quilck-papa*. Breeds from March to October. Common resident, except in Tanintharyi.

2. RAIN QUAIL
Coturnix coromandelica

L 7". A plump little bird with sandy colouration. Found in open country, in cultivation and grassland, usually near villages up to 4,500 feet. Keeps in pairs during breeding season and solitary or in flocks at other times. Call: musical, high-pitched *whit-whit-whit-whit-whit-whit*. Breeds from February to October. Resident, except in Tanintharyi.

3. BLUE-BREASTED QUAIL
Coturnix chinensis

L 6". Male: black and white face with blue-grey sides of head and upper breast, and chestnut belly and under tail coverts. Female: sandy-brownish. Found in grass and scrub of the plains. Seen usually in pairs or coveys. Call: sweet *tiyu-tiyu*. Breeds during the rains. Resident, except in Tanintharyi and W Myanmar.

4. RUFOUS-THROATED PARTRIDGE
Arborophila rufogularis

L 11". An olive-brown bird with rufous throat and grey breast and belly; throat spotted with black; flanks streaked with white and chestnut. Found in forests at 4,000–8,500 feet, usually in a covey of parents and their last brood. Confiding where not pursued. Call: *whu-whu whu-whu* with more rapid *kew-kew kew-kew*. Breeds from March to August. Resident, except in C Myanmar.

1. CHINESE FRANCOLIN
Francolinus pintadeanus

2. RAIN QUAIL
Coturnix coromandelica

3. BLUE-BREASTED QUAIL
Coturnix chinensis

4. RUFOUS-THROATED PARTRIDGE
Arborophila rufogularis

5. RED JUNGLEFOWL
Gallus gallus

L Cock, 30" including 11–13" tail; hen, 17". This bird is the progenitor of domestic poultry. Found in forests, secondary growth, scrub, paddy fields and bamboo-flowering areas up to 5,500 feet. Frequents dense forests during rains and neighbourhood of forest villages in cold season. Male sheds neck plumes in rainy season. Call: like domestic fowl, but higher-pitched with last syllable cut short. Breeds from March to May, somethimes earlier. Distinguished from domestic form by its slate-grey legs and prominent white patch at base of tail in cock. Common resident.

6. KALIJ PHEASANT
Lophura leucomelanos

L 20–29". Light and dark phases occur, both with red facial skin. Found in moist deciduous and evergreen forests up to 6,000 feet, usually in small parties near streams. Keeps to thick cover. Shy. Prefers running to flying when disturbed. Feeds on grains, seeds, leaves and insects. Call: a guttural, harsh crow and a guttural cooing sound. Breeds from March to May. Resident, except in Tanintharyi and E Myanmar.

7. SILVER PHEASANT
Lophura nycthemera

L 20–50" (male tail up to 30" inclusive). Male: blackish or silvery-white. Female: brown or reddish brown. Both sexes have crest and red legs. Found in montane forests at 4,500–9,000 feet, usually in small flocks. Shy, but locally more confiding. Active at dusk and dawn. Call: similar to Kalij Pheasant. Breeds from February to May. Resident in N, C and E Myanmar, and northern Tanintharyi.

8. MRS HUME'S PHEASANT
Syrmaticus humiae

L 24–36" (male tail up to 21" inclusive). Male: chestnut body with long pointed pale grey tail. Female: mottled brown with short tail. Found in montane forests above 4,000 feet. Keeps in small parties on broken, rocky grounds or steep hillsides. Hides in undergrowth in daytimes. Feeds at dusk and dawn. Perches on trees when cornered. Call: a low grunting note. Breeds from March to May. Resident, except in Tanintharyi and SW and S Myanmar.

9. GREY PEACOCK PHEASANT
Polyplectron bicalcaratum

L 22–30". Male: grey-brown body with violet to greenish ocelli. Female: darker plumage with blackish ocelli. Found in evergeen and dense bamboo jungle up to 6,000 feet.Terrestrial and an inveterate skulker, rarely seen even in localities where it is abundant. Seldom flies, but flight low and fast. Monogamous, pairing for life. Call: a loud whistled trew-tree. Breeds in March and April. Resident.

10. GREEN PEAFOWL
Pavo muticus

L 40–96" (male train up to 64" inclusive). A huge bird with brilliant green plumage and narrow upright crest: male has long train. Found in any type of jungle from grass swamps to scrub up to 3,000 feet. Prefers dry open forest on river-banks. Keeps in small parties. Quite confiding where not hunted. Forages on ground and roosts in trees. Polygamous. Call: a loud *kay-yaw kay-yaw*. Breeds from March to May in nests built on ground. Resident.

5. RED JUNGLEFOWL
Gallus gallus

8. MRS HUME'S PHEASANT
Syrmaticus humiae

6. KALIJ PHEASANT
Lophura leucomelanos

7. SILVER PHEASANT
Lophura nycthemera

9. GREY PEACOCK PHEASANT
Polyplectron bicalcaratum

10. GREEN PEAFOWL
Pavo muticus

DUCKS, GEESE Dendrocygnidae, Anatidae

Thirty-four species of ducks and geese occur in Myanmar, but only six are resident. Ducks and geese are aquatic birds with plump bodies, broad, flattened bills and webbed feet. Males have colourful breeding dress; females are usually dull-coloured. In moult, males resemble females. They feed on aquatic plants and animals. Some graze or eat grains in fields. Many are migratory, and they are capable of long flights. They fly with necks fully extended, fast and direct. Most nest in thick vegetation near water, but a few nest in tree holes. They are gregarious.

11. FULVOUS WHISTLING-DUCK
Dendrocygna bicolor
L 20". A light chestnut brown duck with rufescent head and broad black line down back of neck; streaky buffy patch on sides of rufescent neck. Found in marshes and on lakes. Gregarious, generally in small flocks. Call: thin, whistled *k-weeoo* often repeated, uttered mostly in flight. Breeds during the rains in tree holes, sometimes on ground. Resident at low elevations, except in N Myanmar.

12. LESSER WHISTLING-DUCK
Dendrocygna javanica
L 16". A light chestnut brown duck with darker crown, mantle and wings. Sexes alike. Goose-like in appearance with distinctive upright posture. Found in swamps, mangroves and paddy fields; also on lakes. Gregarious and mainly nocturnal. Can run, walk and perch; also a good diver. Call: clear low whistled *whi-whee* incessantly repeated, usually when in flight. Breeds in tree hollows from June to September. Common resident at low elevations.

13. RUDDY SHELDUCK
Tadorna ferruginea
L 25". An orange-chestnut bird with goose-like shape; head, buff-coloured and bill and feet, black. Male has black collar. Found on rivers and lakes in flocks, sometimes in pairs. Rather vocal with a nasal, goose-like honking. The commonest duck of the Ayeyarwaddy river in winter. Winter visitor, October or early November to April.

14. WHITE-WINGED DUCK
Cairina scutulata
L 30". A blackish bird with whitish head and neck, reddish bill and yellow legs. Sexes similar, but bill thicker and plumage glossier in male. Found on streams and in swamps by day, rivers and paddy fields at night. Solitary or paired. Flight exceptionally fast and powerful. Dives and walks well. Feeds mostly at night. Flight call is a prolonged, vibrant series of honks. Breeds from March to September in tree holes. Resident up to 5,000 feet.

15. COMB DUCK
Sarkidiornis melanotos
L 30". Male: head and neck, white with comb at base of upper mandible; rest of upperparts, glossy black. Female: similar but smaller and lacks comb. Found on marshy lakes; also in paddy fields. Solitary or paired, sometimes in small flocks. Flight strong and sustained. Swims and walks well. Feeds on land and in water. Roosts in trees and nests in tree hollows often far from water. Occasionally utters low croaking sounds. Breeds from June to September. Resident at low elevations, except in Tanintharyi.

11. FULVOUS WHISTLING-DUCK
Dendrocygna bicolor

12. LESSER WHISTLING-DUCK
Dendrocygna javanica

13. RUDDY SHELDUCK
Tadorna ferruginea

14. WHITE-WINGED DUCK
Cairina scutulata

15. COMB DUCK
Sarkidiornis melanotos

16. COTTON PYGMY-GOOSE
Nettapus coromandelianus
L 13". Smallest duck with short bill and chunky shape. Male: blackish with greenish gloss. Female: duller and brownish. Found in marshes and paddy fields; also on rivers and canals. Walks only with difficulty. Very confiding when not hunted. Flight, swift and effortless. Feeds on surface and rarely dives. Male has a staccato cackling, usually in flight and female gives a weak quack. Breeds from July to August in tree holes. Resident at low elevations.

17. SPOT-BILLED DUCK
Anas poecilorhyncha
L 24". A blackish duck with yellow-tipped black bill and coral-red feet; sides of head and neck, whitish. Found in marshes; also on rivers and lakes. Keeps in pairs or small flocks, often with other ducks. Call: quack, like domestic duck. Breeds from June to November in nests built on ground, usually near water. Resident at low elevations in C, S and E Myanmar.

18. NORTHERN PINTAIL
Anas acuta
L 22" (Male tail 4" longer). Male: grey with dark chocolate-brown head and neck and elongated, black central tail feathers. Female: mottled brown. Found on rivers, lakes and sea-coasts; also in marshes. Usually seen in flocks. Flight, very swift. Shy but quite confiding where not hunted. Remains at centre of expanses of water during the day and raids ricefields at night. Male utters a low preep, female a weak quack when flushed. Winter visitor, October to mid-February.

19. COMMON TEAL
Anas crecca
L 15". Male; grey with dark chestnut head and dark green band from eye to nape. Female: mottled brown; bright green speculum often visible at rest. Found on lakes and in marshes, usually in large flocks. Flight, very swift and strong. Male utters a soft preep, female a sharp high quack when flushed. Winter visitor, October to March.

BUTTONQUAILS Turnicidae
Three species of buttonquail occur in Myanmar, and all are resident.

Buttonquails are tiny, rounded birds with very short tails. They have only three toes (no hind toe). Females are larger and more richly coloured than males, and play dominant role in courtship. Males incubate the eggs and rear the young. They live in open country, in grass and scrub. They prefer to run, rather than take flight when disturbed. When forced to fly, flight is straight and fast and covers about fifty yards. They feed on insects, seeds and other vegetable matter. They breed year round.

20. YELLOW-LEGGED BUTTONQUAIL
Turnix tanki
L 6½". A sandy-buff bird with yellow bill and legs and black spots on wings. Female has ferruginous collar on hindneck. Found in grassland, scrub and cultivation up to 7,000 feet. Female territorial call is a series of low-pitched hooting notes, gradually increasing in strength and turning into a human-like moan. Resident, but absent in W and N Myanmar.

16. COTTON PYGMY-GOOSE
Nettapus coromandelianus

17. SPOT-BILLED DUCK
Anas poecilorhyncha

18. NORTHERN PINTAIL
Anas acuta

19. COMMON TEAL
Anas crecca

20. YELLOW-LEGGED BUTTONQUAIL
Turnix tanki

21. BARRED BUTTONQUAIL
Turnix suscitator

L 6½". A dark reddish-brown bird with grey bill and feet. Male has bold black barring on breast. Female has black throat and centre of breast. Found in grassland, scrub and cultivations up to 5,000 feet. Often found on edges of farmland. Female territorial call is a series of soft, ventriloquial, reverberating booming notes gradually increasing in volume before ending abruptly. Common resident.

WOODPECKERS Picidae

The woodpeckers are represented in Myanmar by thirty-nine species, of which thirty-eight are resident.

Woodpeckers are arboreal birds and usually cling to tree trunks. Their bills are powerful and straight, and end in a chisel-formed edge. They have small sticky tongues which can be pushed far out of the mouths. Their tongues are used for catching larvae and insects. They feed mostly on wood-boring insects, although many feed on ants on the ground. Their flight is strong and undulating. Many are territorial and sedentary. Males of many species produce a drumming note, particularly during breeding season, by hammering very rapidly with the beak against dead wood. They nest in self-bored holes in trees.

22. SPECKLED PICULET
Picumnus innorminatus

L 4". A tiny, olive-green woodpecker; underparts, whitish with black spots and bars. Found in forest undergrowth and outskirts; partial to bamboo thickets. Usually solitary; often seen together with parties of small babblers. Feeds on ants and larvae, often on fallen trees, but not on the ground. Call: sharp tsit and squeaky *sik-sik-sik*. Breeds from January to April. Resident up to 6,000 feet.

23. GREY-CAPPED WOODPECKER
Dendrocopos canicapillus

L 6". A tiny woodpecker with black and white bars above and dark streaks on breast and belly: male has red streaks on head. Found in forests at all elevations. Active and quick in movements. Usually seen in pairs. Call: short *kik* or *pit* and squeaky *kweek-kweek-kweek*. Breeds from December to April. Resident.

24. RUFOUS WOODPECKER
Celeus brachyurus

L 12". A dark rufous woodpecker with black-barred upper parts; bill, black. Male has red malar patch. Found in forests of the plains and foothills up to 3,000 feet. Feeds on ants and termites on trees and ground. Call: nasal laughing *kweep-kweep-kweep*. Breeds from February to June. Common resident.

25. LESSER YELLOWNAPE
Picus chlorolophus

L 10½". A yellow-crested, green woodpecker with barred underparts. Found in forests of foothills and higher hills up to 6,000 feet; partial to bamboo and scrub-jungle. Solitary or paired. Often seen on forest tracks. Feeds on ground occasionally. Call: far-carrying, plaintive *peee-uu* or *pee-a*. Breeds from March to May. Common resident.

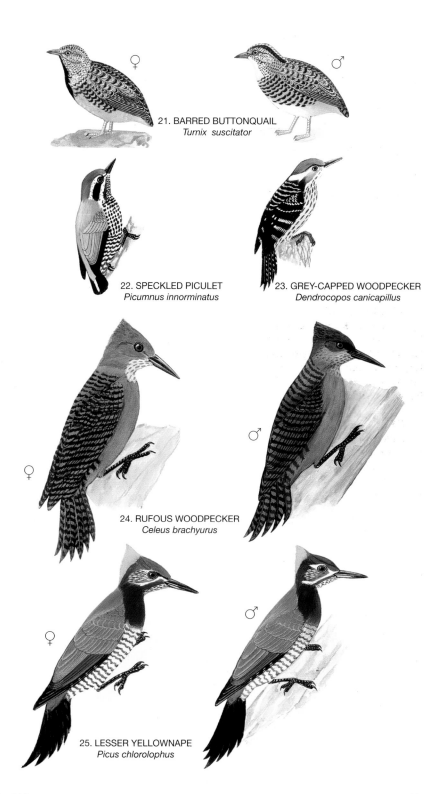

21. BARRED BUTTONQUAIL
Turnix suscitator

22. SPECKLED PICULET
Picumnus innorminatus

23. GREY-CAPPED WOODPECKER
Dendrocopos canicapillus

24. RUFOUS WOODPECKER
Celeus brachyurus

25. LESSER YELLOWNAPE
Picus chlorolophus

26. GREATER YELLOWNAPE
Picus flavinucha

L 13H". A large greenish woodpecker with rufous-brown crown and yellow nuchal crest. Male has yellow throat, streaked below. Female has streaked throat and chestnut malar patch. Found in forests up to 9,000 feet. Feeds in understorey as well as on tree-tops. Seldom descends to ground. Pairs for life. Call: accelerating *kwee-kwee-kwee-kwee-kwi-kwi-wi-wi-wik*. Breeds from February to May. Resident.

27. STREAK-BREASTED WOODPECKER
Picus viridanus

L 12". A yellowish-green woodpecker with bright yellow rump; crown and crest, crimson in male, black in female. Found in coastal scrub and forests up to 5,000 feet. Feeds mostly on ground, ants being its favourite food. Call: explosive *kirrr*. Breeds from February to April. Endemic resident in SW, S, C and south E Myanmar and Tanintharyi.

28. GREY-HEADED WOODPECKER
Picus canus

L 13". A green woodpecker with unmarked underparts; forecrown, red in male, black in female. Found in forests and wooded areas in the plains and foothills ascending to 5,000 feet. Keeps in parties of four to six birds. Feeds on ground or in understorey. Call: short *kik* and *keek-kak-kak-kak*. Breeds from March to June. Resident.

29. COMMON FLAMEBACK
Dinopium javanense

L 12". A golden yellow woodpecker with black and white face pattern; crown, red in male, black in female. Found in well-wooded areas, gardens, coconut groves and cultivations up to 5,000 feet. Usually seen in pairs. Call: *kow* and *kowp-owp-owp-owp* uttered in flight. Breeds from March to June. Common resident.

30. GREATER FLAMEBACK
Chrysocolaptes lucidus

L 13". A golden yellow woodpecker with black and white face pattern; crown, red in male, black with white spots in female. Found in forests, ascending to 4,000 feet. Feeds both on ground and in trees. Call: *kik*. Breeds from March to May. Common resident.

BARBETS Megalaimidae

Myanmar has ten species of Barbet and all are resident.

Barbets are birds of tree-tops. They are heavy-bodied with large heads and stout bills adorned with bristles. They have mostly green plumage with distinctive facial patterns. They are usually solitary, sluggish and slow-moving with heavy dipping flight. They feed on fruits, seeds, figs, buds and nectar. Sometimes several species feed in the same fruiting tree. They lay eggs in tree holes which they excavate.

31. GREAT BARBET
Megalaima virens

L 13". A greenish brown bird with dark blue head, large yellow bill and yellow-streaked underparts. Found in forests of higher hills at 3,000–7,000 feet. Keeps to treetops. A great fruit eater; partial to wild figs. Male territorial call is a strident *kay-oh kay-oh kay-oh*. Breeds from February to April, sometimes in disused woodpecker holes in trees. Common resident.

28. GREY-HEADED WOODPECKER
Picus canus

26. GREATER YELLOWNAPE
Picus flavinucha

29. COMMON FLAMEBACK
Dinopium javanense

30. GREATER FLAMEBACK
Chrysocolaptes lucidus

27. STREAK-BREASTED WOODPECKER
Picus viridanus

31. GREAT BARBET
Megalaima virens

32. LINEATED BARBET
Megalaima lineata

L 11½". A grass-green bird with streaked pale brown head, throat and breast; streaks often not visible in field. Found in wooded areas adjoining forests, gardens and orchards up to 4,000 feet. Avoids towns and villages of the paddy plains. Male territorial call is a very loud, mellow *poo-poh poo-poh poo-poh*. Breeds from February to July. Common resident.

33. GOLDEN-THROATED BARBET
Megalaima franklinii

L 9". A green bird with golden chin and throat and crimson forehead and crown, yellow in between; sides of head streaked. Found in forests at 3,500–7,000 feet. A characteristic bird of hill forests. Very shy. Male territorial call is a very loud, ringing *pukwowk pukwowk pukwowk*. Breeds from February to August. Resident.

34. BLUE-THROATED BARBET
Megalaima asiatica

L 9". A greenish bird with red cap and blue throat and sides of head. Found in wooded areas at 2,000–4,000 feet. A few individuals go up to 6,000 feet. A characteristic bird of teak forests. Generally solitary, but may be found in groups. Male territorial call is a very loud *took-arook took-arook took-arook*. Breeds from March to July. Common resident.

35. COPPERSMITH BARBET
Megalaima haemacephala

L 6". A green bird with red forehead and yellow chin and throat. Found in wooded areas, gardens and cities up to 3,000 feet. A common bird of the plains; also common in teak forests. Solitary. Male territorial call is a very loud, resonant *tonk tonk tonk*. Breeds from February to May. Common resident.

HORNBILLS Bucerotidae

The hornbills are represented in Myanmar by nine species and all are resident.

Hornbills are large forest birds with huge bills which bear casques. They feed mainly on fruits, and also take insects and small animals. They live in pairs and mate for life. Outside breeding season, some species roost communally in large numbers. They fly long distances over forest in flocks for food. They nest in tree holes, in which the female remains sealed until the young are partially grown.

36. ORIENTAL PIED HORNBILL
Anthracoceros albirostris

L 27". A black bird with white face patch, white belly and white-tipped outer tail feathers. Bill and large casque, ivory with black mark which differs in pattern in male and female. Found in forest, forest edge and scrubby woodland throughout the plains and foothills up to 4,000 feet. Usually seen in small flocks of about half a dozen, but sometimes many more birds. Call: high-pitched *kleng-keng kek-kek-kek-kek-kek* and *ayip-yip yip yip*. Breeds from March to May. Resident.

32. LINEATED BARBET
Megalaima lineata

33. GOLDEN-THROATED BARBET
Megalaima franklinii

34. BLUE-THROATED BARBET
Megalaima asiatica

35. COPPERSMITH BARBET
Megalaima haemacephala

36. ORIENTAL PIED HORNBILL
Anthracoceros albirostris

Birds of Myanmar

37. GREAT HORNBILL
Buceros bicornis
L 47". A large black bird with white neck and tail; face, black; bill and casque, yellowish; white patch on wings; black, subterminal band on tail. Eyes, reddish in male and whitish in female. Found in forests of the foothills up to 4,000 feet. Pairs for life. Collects into flocks of six to eighteen birds outside breeding season. Omnivorous, but mainly eats fruits. Call: barking roar, *wharr*. Breeds from January to April. Resident.

38. WREATHED HORNBILL
Aceros undulatus
L 40". A large black bird with dull yellowish bill and white tail. Male has brownish-white sides of crown, neck and upper breast, dark brown nape and hind-neck and yellow gular pouch. Female has all-black head and neck and blue gular pouch. Found in forests up to 5,000 feet. Keeps in pairs or small flocks; sometimes seen in large flocks. Call: loud, rather breathless *kuk-kwehk*. Breeds from February to August. Resident.

HOOPOE Upupidae
The hoopoe, the only species of this family, occurs in Myanmar.

The hoopoe is a slender-bodied bird with erectile crest and long, decurved bill. It feeds entirely on the ground, probing soft ground and turning over leaves and litter for insects, caterpillars and grubs. It breeds in tree holes. Sexes are alike.

39. COMMOM HOOPOE
Upupa epops
L 12". A pinkish bird with a black-tipped crest usually carried flat on head. Found in open cultivated country, grassy lawns and dry bamboo jungle up to 5,000 feet. Crest erected when excited or alarmed, or on settling for a moment. Solitary or in small noisy parties. Flies away into trees when disturbed. Flight low and plunging, but can be very sustained. Call: low, soft *hoop-hoop-hoop*. Breeds from March to June. Resident.

TROGONS Trogonidae
Myanmar has four species of trogon and all are resident.

Trogons are beautifully coloured birds with a short, broad bill and a very broad, square-cut tail. They have soft fluffy plumage. Males have brighter plumage than females. They are shy, rather quiet and solitary (sometimes seen in pairs). They perch in an upright posture usually in the middle storey of forest and feed on insects which they take on short flights from perch. They lay eggs in tree hollows.

40. ORANGE-BREASTED TROGON
Harpectes oreskios
L 12". An orange-yellow bird; head and breast, greenish-tinged in male and greyish-tinged in female. Found in moist and evergreen forests and thin tree and bamboo jungle up to 4,000 feet. Possibly more terrestrial. Often seen in mixed-species feeding flocks. Feeds chiefly on bugs and beetles. Male territorial call is *teu-teu-teu* or *tu-tau tau tau*. Breeds from February to April. Resident, except in N and C Myanmar.

37. GREAT HORNBILL
Buceros bicornis

♀

♂

38. WREATHED HORNBILL
Aceros undulatus

♀

♂

40. ORANGE-BREASTED TROGON
Harpectes oreskios

♀

39. COMMOM HOOPOE
Upupa epops

♂

41. RED-HEADED TROGON
Harpactes erythrocephalus

L 13½". A reddish bird with a whitish crescent across breast. Found in forests from the plains to 6,000 feet. Male has red head and breast, female brown head and russet breast.A typical bird of deep forest. Quiet, silent and fearless. Active in mornings and evenings. When alarmed, flies a short distance and settles down quietly again. Mainly insectivorous, but also takes leaves, seeds and other vegetable matter. Male territorial call is a *taup taup taup*. Breeds from March to May. Resident, usually above 2,000 feet.

ROLLERS Coraciidae

The rollers are represented in Myanmar by two species and both are resident.

Rollers have a thick body, a large head and a powerful bill. They somewhat resemble the crows in form but are more brightly coloured, with dark purplish or bluish plumage. They live up in treetops where they sit on a branch on the lookout for prey, usually large insects, grasshoppers, beetles, lizards, frogs, small rodents etc. They are solitary or paired. They often breed in colonies and lay their eggs in tree hollows, cliff crevices and earth holes.

42. INDIAN ROLLER
Coracias benghalensis

L 13". A dark purplish brown bird when perched; shows a sudden flash of blue wings and tail when it takes flight. Found in open country and cities up to 5,000 feet. Perches on elevated, exposed branches or ruined buildings or heaps of stones; also on telegraphic wires. Mainly active in mornings and evenings. Frogs form a large proportion of diet, but also catches insects both in flight and on the ground. Call: *kyak*. Breeds from March to May. Common resident.

43. DOLLARBIRD
Eurystomus orientalis

L 12". A blackish bird with red bill; shows broad silvery patch (like silver dollar) on the wing in flight. Found in forests of foothills up to 4,000 feet. A characteristic bird of teak forests of Bago Yoma. Normally a sluggish bird, but active when excited. Crepuscular. Rather shy. May often be seen perched on bare branches. Call: *kreck kreck, kak, kiak* etc. Breeds from March to May. Resident.

KINGFISHERS Alcedinidae, Halcyonidae, Cerylidae

Fifteen species of kingfisher occur in Myanmar, and fourteen are resident.

Kingfishers are large-headed birds with long, pointed bills and compact bodies; they have short legs and tails. Most are brilliantly coloured. Many stay close to water, but some are forest birds. Some species feed on fish; some, on insects and terrestrial animals. Most nest in tunnels, but some species nest in tree hollows. They are usually solitary, but sometimes seen in pairs.

44. COMMON KINGFISHER
Alcedo atthis

L 7". A small bluish green kingfisher; underparts, orange-rufous. Found in open country, in mangroves and marshes; also on lakes and waterways up to 6,000 feet. Territorial. Solitary. Flight, direct, fast and strong. Sometimes hovers over open water. Feeds on fish. Utters usually two or three shrill, high-pitched piping notes particularly in flight. Breeds from March to June; sometimes irregular. Common resident.

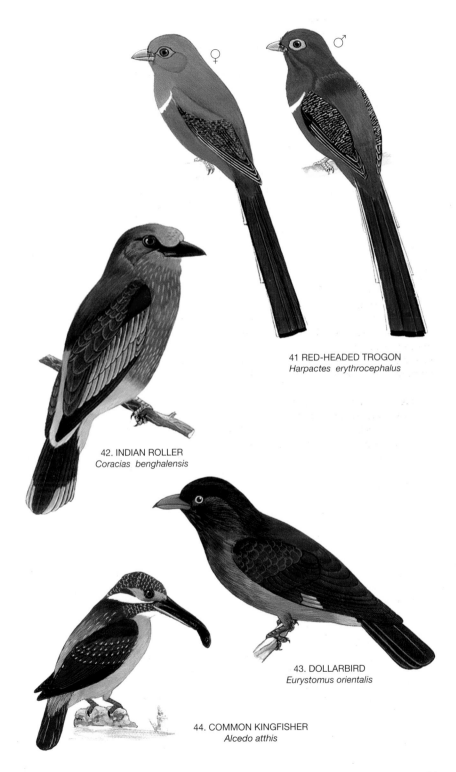

♀ ♂

41 RED-HEADED TROGON
Harpactes erythrocephalus

42. INDIAN ROLLER
Coracias benghalensis

43. DOLLARBIRD
Eurystomus orientalis

44. COMMON KINGFISHER
Alcedo atthis

45. STORK-BILLED KINGFISHER
Halcyon capensis

L 14½". A bluish kingfisher; underparts ochraceous. Found in open country, in swamp forests, mangroves and paddyfields and on rivers and wooded streams up to 4,000 feet. A typical bird of streams in teak forests of Bago Yoma. Flight very powerful. Not shy. Often seen far from water. Feeds on fish. Territorial call is a melancholy whistled *iuu iuu iuu*. Breeds from February to May. Common resident.

46. WHITE-THROATED KINGFISHER
Halcyon smyrnensis

L 11". A bluish kingfisher: throat and upper breast, white; head and lower under body brownish. Found in the plains and foothills in open areas near water. Often seen perched on telephone wires and dead trees overhanging water or paddyfields. Often found far from water. A noisy bird. Feeds on insects, frogs, lizards etc. Territorial call is a loud whinnying *klilililililii*. Breeds during hot weather, mostly in April. Common resident, up to 5,000 feet.

47. BLACK-CAPPED KINGFISHER
Halcyon pileata

L 12". A deep blue kingfisher with black cap, bright red bill and narrow white collar on neck. Found mainly on coast and tidal creeks, also inland wooded streams, sometimes in paddy fields. Flight powerful, buoyant and direct. Feeds mainly on fish, also on some other small creatures. Call: ringing, cackling, *kikikikikiki*. Breeds in hot weather. Resident in Tanintharyi and W and S Myanmar.

48. COLLARED KINGFISHER
Todiramphus chloris

L 9½". A pale green kingfisher with white collar and underparts; upperside of wings, entirely blue. Found in coastal areas. Fairly common round the islands of Myeik Archipelago. A noisy confiding bird, often living near villages; sometimes nests in houses. Feeds on shellfish and small reptiles. Call: *kick kyew, kick kyew*. Breeds from December to August. Resident.

49. PIED KINGFISHER
Ceryle rudis

L 12". A black and white kingfisher with a short crest. Found on rivers, canals, streams, lakes and flooded areas below 3,000 feet. A familiar bird of the Ayeyarwaddy River. Spends much of its time perching on bare branches overhanging the water, waiting to plunge on prey. Frequently hovers with bill pointed downwards. Feeds on small fish. Call: *kwik or kik*, also *chirruk chirruk*. Breeds from October to December. Resident.

BEE-EATERS Meropidae

The bee-eaters are represented in Myanmar by five species, and all are resident.

Bee-eaters are slender-bodied birds with long, curved, narrow bills and long pointed wings. Plumages are predominantly green. They feed on bees and insects, and lay eggs in burrows or tunnels dug in steep earthern banks, often in colonies. Sexes are similar or nearly so. Merops species are mainly found in open country and are gregarious. Nyctyornis species are forest-dwellers and are solitary or paired.

50. BLUE-BEARDED BEE-EATER
Nyctyornis athertoni

L 14". A greenish bird with shaggy blue patch on throat and breast, and yellowish belly streaked with green. Found in forests and wooded areas up to 5,000 feet. Solitary or in

45. STORK-BILLED KINGFISHER
Halcyon capensis

47. BLACK-CAPPED KINGFISHER
Halcyon pileata

46. WHITE-THROATED KINGFISHER
Halcyon smyrnensis

49. PIED KINGFISHER
Ceryle rudis

48. COLLARED KINGFISHER
Todiramphus chloris

50. BLUE-BEARDED BEE-EATER
Nyctyornis athertoni

pairs. Feeds little on wing. Searches leaves and flowers for insects, clambering about with slow, awkward movements. Call: *grrew-grrew-grrew*, also *kow kow kow kow kow kow*. Breeds from March to August. Resident.

51. GREEN BEE-EATER
Merops orientalis
L 8". A green bird with elongated central tail feathers: crown and nape, coppery brown; throat, green with a black gorget. Found in open country up to 5,000 feet. Most commonly seen from train windows, owing to its habit of perching on telephone wires. Sometimes found in large groups near villages. Call: *tree-tree-tree-tree* constantly in flight. Breeds from March to May. Common resident.

52. BLUE-TAILED BEE-EATER
Merops philippinus
L 12". A greenish bird with yellow upper throat and black eye-line. Found in open country, in mangroves and flooded areas; also on river banks and flooded paddy plains. Partial to water. Spends more time on wing than other bee-eaters. Flight strong, fast and graceful. Sometimes seen in large parties. Call: *rillip-rillip-rillip* in flight. Breeds from February to May, usually in colonies. Resident.

53. CHESTNUT-HEADED BEE-EATER
Merops leschenaulti
L 8½". A greenish bird with yellow throat and light chestnut crown, nape and upper back. Found in forests, frequenting glades and clearings; also roads and mule paths in the hills up to 6,000 feet. A typical bird of teak forests of Bago Yoma. Sociable, often in large flocks. Call: *prru-uip, pruik, churit* or *djewy* in flight. Breeds from February to June. Resident.

CUCKOOS Cuculidae
Myanmar has twenty-three species of cuckoos, of which eighteen are resident.

The Myanmar cuckoos can be grouped into two types: parasitic and non-parasitic.

The parasitic cuckoos include Clamator, Hierococcyx, Cuculus, Cacomantis, Chrysococcyx, Surniculus and Eudynamys. They lay their eggs in other birds' nests and do not take part in raising the young. They are generally solitary and arboreal, hiding in leafy branches of trees. They feed primarily on insects. They have "songs" during breeding season.

The Phaenicophaeus are non-parasitic cuckoos. They are large arboreal birds with long tails. They are often found in pairs and are rather silent. They seldom fly, climbing about among the foliage. They feed on insects and small vertebrates and build their own nests in thick foliage.

54. LARGE HAWK CUCKOO
Hierococcyx sparverioides
L 16". A brownish-grey bird with rufous breast and white underparts; breast usually mottled and streaked with white and grey, and underparts barred with brown. Found in forest at all elevations, more abundant in higher hills. Call: loud, whistled brain *fever* or *pi-pee-ha*, repeated over and over. Single egg laid in nests of laughingthrushes, babblers and spiderhunters. Resident.

51. GREEN BEE-EATER
Merops orientalis

52. BLUE-TAILED BEE-EATER
Merops philippinus

53. CHESTNUT-HEADED BEE-EATER
Merops leschenaulti

54. LARGE HAWK CUCKOO
Hierococcyx sparverioides

Birds of Myanmar

23

55. INDIAN CUCKOO
Cuculus micropterus
L 13". A brownish-grey bird with grey head, throat and upper breast; rest of underparts whitish with black bars. Female has rufous tinge on breast. Found in forests at all elevations, commoner in higher hills. Call: melodious, far-reaching *whi-whi-whi-wu* or *wa-wa-wa-wu*. Eggs laid in nests of drongos and broadbills. Resident.

56. PLAINTIVE CUCKOO
Cacomantis merulinus
L.9". A dark brownish grey bird with rufous-buff underparts. Found in lightly wooded country, scrub, gardens and cultivations up to 6,000 feet. Favours marshland. Retreats to higher hills in breeding season. Call: *tay-ta-tee* or *tay-ta-ta-tay*. Lays eggs in nests of tailorbirds, prinias, hill warblers etc. Common resident, mostly in lowlands.

57. DRONGO CUCKOO
Surniculus lugubris
L 9¼". A glossy black bird with square tail and white bands on under tail coverts. Found in open forests and bamboo jungle below 4000 feet. Flight undulating. Call: fairly, quick *pi pi pi pi pi*. Eggs laid in nests of babblers and tits. Sparingly distributed throughout the country. Resident.

58. ASIAN KOEL
Eudynamys scolopacea
L .17". Males are glossy black; females, dark brown with buff bars and spots. Found in open forests, scrub, gardens and cultivations up to 4,000 feet. Seldom seen; hides in thick foliage of tall trees. Earliest calls heard in February, silent during the rains and after. Call: very loud *ko-el*. Lays eggs in nests of house crow. Common resident.

59. GREEN-BILLED MALKOHA
Phaenicophaeus tristis
L.22" (including 15" tail). A grey bird with oily green wings and tail, and bright red eye-patch. Found in forests, secondary growth, scrub and coastal areas; often, in out-skirts of towns and villages up to 5,000 feet. Typically a forest bird. Flight weak; seldom flies, hopping among branches. May mate for life, the pair never separating through-out the year. Call: clucking, croaking *ko ko ko*. Breeds from March to September. Com-mon resident.

COUCALS Centropodidae
The coucals are represented in Myanmar by three species, and all are resident.

Coucals are large terrestrial birds of the ground, grass and bushes. They have long tails and thickish bills. Their flight is rather weak. They feed on terrestrial insects and small vertebrates, and build nests in low bushes with grass.

60. GREATER COUCAL
Centropus sinensis
L 21". A big blackish bird with chestunt wings. Found in grassland, mangroves, second growth and scrub up to 4,000 feet. Prefers cover beside streams and swamps. Seen on ground, walking and picking up beetles, grasshoppers, and lizards. Also catches snakes and small birds. Ascends trees or bushes by hopping up from branch to branch. Fond of basking in the sun on top of bush after rain. Call: deep, hollow *hoop hoop hoop hoop*. Breeds during the rains. Builds nest in bush or tall grass. Common resident.

56. PLAINTIVE CUCKOO
Cacomantis merulinus

55. INDIAN CUCKOO
Cuculus micropterus

57. DRONGO CUCKOO
Surniculus lugubris

♀

58. ASIAN KOEL
Eudynamys scolopacea

♂

59. GREEN-BILLED MALKOHA
Phaenicophaeus tristis

60. GREATER COUCAL
Centropus sinensis

61. LESSER COUCAL
Centropus bengalensis
L 15". A smaller blackish bird with paler chestnut wings. Found in second growth, scrub, grassland and marshes up to 6,000 feet. A typical bird of extensive areas of *kaing* grass or *thetke*. Call: *whoop whoop whoop whoop whoop, kok-kok kok-kok kok-kok kok-kok, kok-kok-oo kok-kok-oo*. Breeds during the rains. Common resident.

PARROTS Psittacidae
Eight species of parrot occur in Myanmar, and all are resident.

Parrots are popular cage birds. They have large heads and short, strongly hooked bills. Wings are narrow and pointed, and tails are long and narrow. Legs are short. Plumage is mostly green.

Parrots in Myanmar differ little in their habits. They live in flocks outside breeding season, and feed on fruits, nuts, seeds etc. in trees; sometimes on crops. They roost in trees, sometimes together with crows and mynas. Most species breed in hot weather, laying eggs in tree holes, natural or excavated. They pair for life.

62. VERNAL HANGING PARROT
Loriculus vernalis
L 5½". A small green parakeet with red bill, rump and upper tail coverts, and yellowish feet; tail, short. Found in forests, secondary growth and clearings in moist and ever-green forests. Normally quiet, and easily overlooked. Travels in groups, making short circular flights from the tops of tall trees. Hangs upside down when sleeping and often when resting. Feeds on flowers, fruits and berries. Call: squeaky *tee-sip* or *pi-zeez-eet* usually in flight. Breeds from January to April. Resident, except in N and W Myanmar.

63. ALEXANDRINE PARAKEET
Psittacula eupatria
L 20". A green parakeet with red bill and maroon shoulder patch; male has blackich necklet extending into pinkish collar on back of neck. Found in forests of the plains and indaing forests below 3,000 feet. Rather shy. Call: *trrrieuw, ke-ah, keeak, graaak graaak*. Breeds from December to March. Resident.

64. ROSE-RINGED PARAKEET
Psittacula krameri
L 16½". A green parakeet with red bill; male has blackish necklet and pinkish collar, but lacks maroon shoulder patch. Found in light forests and cultivations in the plains and uplands of the central Dry Zone. Call: variable. *kee-ak kee-ak kee-ak, kreh kreh kreh,chee chee*. Breeds from February to May. Resident, except in N Myanmar and Tanintharyi.

65. GREY-HEADED PARAKEET
Psittacula finschii
L 16". A green parakeet with slate-grey head, black throat and red bill; male has red shoulder patch. Found in forests and secondary growth up to 3,500 feet. More of a forest bird in hilly regions than other parrots. A characteristic bird of teak forests of Bago Yoma. Call: *dreet dreet, sweet sweet, swit*. Breeds from January to March Resident.

61. LESSER COUCAL
Centropus bengalensis

♀ ♂

62. VERNAL HANGING PARROT
Loriculus vernalis

♀ ♂

63. ALEXANDRINE PARAKEET
Psittacula eupatria

65. GREY-HEADED PARAKEET
Psittacula finschii

64. ROSE-RINGED PARAKEET
Psittacula krameri

66. BLOSSOM-HEADED PARAKEET
Psittacula roseata
L 13½". A green parakeet with bi-coloured bill and reddish shoulder patch; male has rosy-pink face, black throat and neck-collar and voilet crown and nape; female has dull grey-violet head and no black collar. Found in forests and secondary growth below 3,000 feet. Frequents cultivations and outskirts of forests. Flight fast and direct. Call: *pwi, driii*. Breeds from January to April. Resident, except in N Myanmar.

67. RED-BREASTED PARAKEET
Psittacula alexandri
L 14". A green parakeet with black bar across forehead and orange-pink breast; bill, red in male, black in female. Found in forests and second growth below 6,000 feet. A characteristic bird of teak forests of Bago Yoma. Feeds on shoots, berries, fruits and seeds. Attracted to teak trees when leaves begin to sprout; nips off leaves as it settles. Call: *ek ek, kaink*. Breeds from January to March. Common resident.

SWIFTS, Apodidae
Myanmar has thirteen species of swift, and nine are resident.

Swifts are small birds with long, narrow wings and small, weak feet. They spend much of their time on the wing. They never perch on trees or wires like swallows. They cling to vertical surfaces with their short-clawed toes for rest. They are gregarious, and feed exclusively on flying insects. Sexes are alike.

68. EDIBLE-NEST SWIFTLET
Collocalia fuciphaga
L 5". A blackish bird with notched tail. Found in coastal areas, offshore islands, forests, open country and towns. Nests mainly around coasts and offshore islets in limestone caves and forages inland over forests and open areas. Breeds from February to April. Nest, edible and white, and widely used as a medicine. Common resident at low elevations in S Myanmar.

69. ASIAN PALM SWIFT
Cypsiurus balasiensis
L 5". A dark brown bird with sharply pointed wings and slender tail which appears pointed when closed and deeply forked when spread. Found in open country, usually near palms up to 5,000 feet. Nests and roosts on palm fronds. Call: *sisisi-soo-soo* or *deedle-ee-dee*. Breeds from March to August. Common resident, mostly in lowlands.

70. FORK-TAILED SWIFT
Apus pacificus
L 7½". A blackish bird with white throat and rump. Found in forests and open country. Flight very powerful. May often be seen over water in pursuit of insects. Nests in buildings or on cliffs. Breeding colonies in thousands recorded in the cave at the Gokhteik railway viaduct. Call: *sreee*. Breeds from April to July. Resident in E Myanmar and migrant over rest of the country.

71. HOUSE SWIFT
Apus affinis
L 6". A smaller blackish bird with white throat and rump. Found in cliffs, caves, rocky islets and cities up to 6,000 feet. Feeds mainly over open areas. Nests in buildings or on cliffs. Nests in large buildings in Yangon, including the Office of the Ministers and the City Hall. Call: *der-der-der-dit-der-diddidoo, sik-sik-sik-sik sik-sik sik-sik-sik-sik*. Breeds all year. Common resident, usually in lowlands.

66. BLOSSOM-HEADED PARAKEET
Psittacula roseata

67. RED-BREASTED PARAKEET
Psittacula alexandri

68. EDIBLE-NEST SWIFTLET
Collocalia fuciphaga

69. ASIAN PALM SWIFT
Cypsiurus balasiensis

70. FORK-TAILED SWIFT
Apus pacificus

71. HOUSE SWIFT
Apus affinis

TREESWIFTS Hemiprocnidae

Three species of treeswift occur in Myanmar, and all are resident.
Treeswifts are closely related to true swifts, but they are more colourful and less aerial in habits. They are somewhat gregarious, and sexes differ slightly. Their tails are deeply forked. They perch and nest in trees.

72. CRESTED TREESWIFT
Hemiprocne coronata
L 9". A blue-grey bird with darker glossy wings and tall, pointed crest; male has chestnut cheek patch. Found in forest edge, secondary growth, semi-open country and gardens up to 4,000 feet. Keeps in small parties. Often perches on trees, sitting upright with its crest erect, and hawking insects. Call: *ke-kyew, kip-kEE-kep*. Breeds from March to June. Resident.

OWLS Tytonidae, Strigidae

The Owls are represented in Myanmar by twenty-five species, of which twenty-two are resident.
Owls are nocturnal birds of prey. They have hooked bills and powerful talons. Their heads are big, eyes large and directed forward and plumage, soft. Owing to soft, loose plumage, their flight is noiseless. They are solitary. Most remain hidden by day although some hunt regularly in broad daylight. Many nest in tree hollows, a few in crevices of buildings. Sexes are alike with females slightly larger.

73. BARN OWL
Tyto alba
L 13½". A golden-buff owl with white underparts and heart-shaped facial disc. Found in cultivated areas, cities and buildings throughout the plains. Truly nocturnal, feeding throughout the night and roosting by day in a building or tree hole. Flight, strong and silent. Feeds mainly on mice and rats. Call: a loud screech. Breeds from November to March. Resident in C, S and E Myanmar.

74. MOUNTAIN SCOPS OWL
Otus spilocephalus
L 8". A small rufous horned owl with yellow eyes. Found in moist and evergreen forests up to 7,000 feet. Commoner in mountains. Lives mainly close to the ground. Strictly nocturnal. Call: whistled *toot-toot* or *plew-plew*. Breeds from February to June. Common resident, except in N Myanmar.

75. ORIENTAL SCOPS OWL
Otus sunia
L 7½". A tufted greyish brown to rufous owl with yellow eyes; bold black streaks on underparts. Found in forests and secondary growth of the plains and foothills up to 5,000 feet. Sleeps in thick foliage in daytime. Call: *throaty toink tonk-ta-tonk*. Breeds from February to June. Resident.

76. COLLARED SCOPS OWL
Otus bakkamoena
L 9". A small greyish brown owl with bright buff nuchal collar. Found in forests, secondary growth and gardens from the plains to higher hills up to 7,000 feet. Entirely nocturnal. May be seen near isolated houses close to trees. Call: soft, mellow *hoo-o*. Breeds from January to April. Common resident, mostly in lowlands.

♂ ♀

72. CRESTED TREESWIFT
Hemiprocne coronata

73. BARN OWL
Tyto alba

74. MOUNTAIN SCOPS OWL
Otus spilocephalus

75. ORIENTAL SCOPS OWL
Otus sunia

76. COLLARED SCOPS OWL
Otus bakkamoena

77. BROWN FISH OWL
Ketupa zeylonensis
L 21". A large sandy-brown owl with golden yellow eyes. Found on forested streams and lakes and in paddy fields. Sleeps by day in trees and on the ground. Less nocturnal. Feeds mainly on fish and crabs. Flight strong, fast and silent. Call: deep, hollow *hu-who-hu* or *hup-hup-hu*. Breeds from November to March. Resident.

78. BROWN WOOD OWL
Strix leptogrammica
L 16–22". A large chocolate-brown owl without horns. Found in forests of foothills and higher hills up to 8,500 feet. Common in Bago Yoma. A vigorously courageous bird, preying on creatures up to the size of pheasants, including squirrels. Call: deep, musical *goke, goke-galoo*. Breeds from January to March. Lays eggs in tree hollows or interstices of ficus-bound trees. Resident.

79. COLLARED OWLET
Glaucidium brodei
L 6½". A tiny owl with imitation facial pattern on nape and hindneck. Plumage variable, but mostly deep rufous barred with black. Found in forests at all elevations to 10,000 feet. Jerks tail when excited. Call: rather metallic *tonk-ta-tonk-tonk*. Breeds from March to July. Common resident, except in SW Myanmar.

80. ASIAN BARRED OWLET
Glaucidium cuculoides
L 9". A dark brown owl with yellow eyes: upperparts barred with rufous buff; breast barred dark brown; belly and flanks broadly streaked rufous brown. Found in forests, second growth and scrub up to 4,000 feet. Probably the most diurnal of all owls. Takes refuge in deep cover during heat of day. Feeds mainly on insects caught in flight or on the ground. Call: variable, including long, descending, trill, *wu'u'u'u'u'u'u'u'u'u'*. Breeds from February to May. Common resident.

81. SPOTTED OWLET
Athene brama
L 8". A grey brown owl with white spots on upperparts and broad, broken bars on underparts. Found in open country in cultivations and buildings. Noisy and very confiding. Often found near villages. Flight rapid, silent and undulating.Feeds almost exclusively on insects.Call: variable, including *zi-gwet*. Breeds from February to April. Resident, usually in lowlands in W, C, S and E Myanmar.

82. BROWN HAWK OWL
Ninox scutulata
L 12". A dark brown owl with coarse brown streaks on underparts and white patch between eyes; tail, long. Found in forests, secondary growth and cultivations in the plains and foothills up to 4,000 feet, sometimes near villages. Feeds mainly on insects, but also takes small reptiles and other creatures. Inactive during daytime. Call: mellow whistle, *coo-oo*. Breeds from March to June. Common resident.

NIGHTJARS Eurostopodidae, Caprimulgidae
Five species of nightjar occur in Myanmar and all are resident.

Nightjars are nocturnal birds. They have soft, beautifully mottled plumage, long tails, long slender pointed wings, large eyes and small and weak bills and feet. They are solitary, and spend daytime on ground or perched lengthwise on a branch. They feed on insects, and lay eggs on ground without making a nest.

78. BROWN WOOD OWL
Strix leptogrammica

77. BROWN FISH OWL
Ketupa zeylonensis

80. ASIAN BARRED OWLET
Glaucidium cuculoides

79. COLLARED OWLET
Glaucidium brodei

81. SPOTTED OWLET
Athene brama

82. BROWN HAWK OWL
Ninox scutulata

83. GREAT EARED NIGHTJAR
Eurostopodus macrotis

L 16". A large dark brown nightjar with ear-tufts. Sexes alike. Found in forests, scrub and secondary growth up to 4,000 feet. A common bird of teak forests in Bago Yoma. Sometimes seen in small parties. Flies with slow leisurely wingbeats.Often feeds high in air at treetop level. Call: loud, musical *pee-weyew* on the wing. Breeds from January to April. Resident.

84. LARGE-TAILED NIGHTJAR
Caprimulgus macrurus

L 12". A buffish-brown bird; male has white patches on wings and tail; patches buff in female. Found in teak and hill forests, open wooded areas, scrub and cultivations up to 7,000 feet. The commonest forest nighjar in Myanmar. Call: loud *chounk chounk chounk chounk chounk*. Breeds from February to May, mainly in March. Common resident.

85. INDIAN NIGHTJAR
Caprimulgus asiaticus

L 9". A smaller buffish brown bird with pale eyebrow and nuchal collar. Sexes alike. Found in dry scrub and open areas with grass below 3,000 feet. Common in Dry Zone of C Myanmar. Commonly seen around Yangon in October and November. Tends to perch on posts rather than in trees. Captures insects in flight as well as on the ground. Call: *chuk chuk chuk chuk-kkkroo*. Breeds from February to June. Resident, except in N Myanmar.

PIGEONS, DOVES Columbidae

This family is represented in Myanmar by twenty-six species, of which twenty-five are resident.

Pigeons and doves are plump-bodied birds with small heads and short bills and legs. They fly long distances for food, and their flights are strong and direct.

Green pigeons (*Treron*) are easily recognized by green plumage. Sexes differ, often with males beautifully coloured. They are stoutly built birds, and are strictly arboreal. They are gregarious outside breeding season. They feed on fruits,especially figs and nest in trees.

Wood pigeons (*Columba*) and doves are ground-feeding birds with predominantly brown plumage. They eat primarily seeds and also some berries and fruits. They are less gregarious than green pigeons. They nest in trees, bushes and sometimes buildings.

The young are fed with pigeon milk, a thick semi-liquid formed in the crop of the parents.

86. ROCK PIGEON
Columba livia

L 13". A blue-grey pigeon with two dark wing bars. Normally seen in flocks in cities in semi-domesticated state. Wild colonies were reported to occur on the coastal plains of Rakhine and along the cliffs of the Ayeyarwaddy River between Bagan and Yenangyaung. Song is a soft guttural *oo-roo-coo*. Breeds throughout the year. Common resident.

83. GREAT EARED NIGHTJAR
Eurostopodus macrotis

84. LARGE-TAILED NIGHTJAR
Caprimulgus macrurus

85. INDIAN NIGHTJAR
Caprimulgus asiaticus

86. ROCK PIGEON
Columba livia

87. ORIENTAL TURTLE-DOVE
Streptopelia orientalis

L 12½". A vinous-brown dove with a patch of black and blue-grey scale markings on sides of neck. Found in forests, secondary growth and scrub from the plains to higher hills up to 7,000 feet. Likes to feed on fallen grains of rice after the harvest. May collect in a flock, but behave individually. Call: dull, sleepy *croo croo croo croooo*. Breeds from February to April. Resident.

88. SPOTTED DOVE
Streptopelia chinensis

L 12". A brownish dove with white-spotted black collar on hind neck. Found in open forest, open country, secondary growth, cultivations and gardens up to 6,000 feet. The most popular pet pigeon. Often seen along watercourses. Normally does not collect in flocks. Call: *cuck-croo-cuck, cuck-croo croo-oo-cuck*. Breeds throughout the year. Common resident.

89. RED COLLARED DOVE
Streptopelia tranquebarica

L 9". Male, brick-red and female, dull brown. Both have narrow black collar on hindneck. Found in open country, scrub, second growth and cultivations. Gregarious and shows little fear of man. Call: deep *cru-u-u-u-u cru-u-u-u-u cru-u-u-u-u cru-u-u-u-u*. Breeds from February to August. Builds nest in trees. Common resident at low elevations.

90. EMERALD DOVE
Chalcophaps indica

L 10". A green dove with reddish vinous face and underparts. Male has conspicuous white forehead and eyebrow. Found in forests, secondary growth and cultivations up to 8,000 feet. Solitary, but sometimes in small parties. Shy, quiet and alert. Feeds mainly on seeds on the ground. Call: soft, far-carrying *cu-oo*. Breeds from January to June, earlier in the south, later in the north. Resident.

91. THICK-BILLED GREEN PIGEON
Treron curvirostra

L 10½". A green pigeon with red-based thick greenish yellow bill; male has maroon mantle and chestnut under tail coverts. Found in forests up to 4,000 feet. Primarily arboreal, descending to ground only to drink. When alarmed, "freezes" motionless. Normally solitary or in small groups. Call: hoarse *goo-goo* when foraging. Breeds from January to September. Resident.

92. YELLOW-FOOTED GREEN PIGEON
Treron phoenicoptera

L 13". A greenish grey bird with bright yellow olive band around neck and upper breast, and yellow feet. Found in cultivations, scrub, gardens and drier open forests throughout the plains and foothills, ascending to 4,000 feet. Chiefly a Dry Zone bird. Normally solitary or in small groups. Call: beautiful, soft whistle of about ten melodious notes. Breeds from March to June. Resident.

93. GREEN IMPERIAL PIGEON
Ducula aenea

L 17". A pale grey bird with dull, bronze-green upperparts, grey bill, crimson cere and red feet. Found in moist forests of foothills up to 3,000 feet; sometimes in mangroves. Frequents tall trees, often near wide streams. Flight strong and fast. Extremely shy. Call: lovely, deep *click-hroooo*. Breeds from March to June. Resident.

87. ORIENTAL TURTLE-DOVE
Streptopelia orientalis

88. SPOTTED DOVE
Streptopelia chinensis

♂

89. RED COLLARED DOVE
Streptopelia tranquebarica

♀

♀

91. THICK-BILLED GREEN PIGEON
Treron curvirostra

90. EMERALD DOVE
Chalcophaps indica

♂

92. YELLOW-FOOTED GREEN PIGEON
Treron phoenicoptera

93. GREEN IMPERIAL PIGEON
Ducula aenea

94. MOUNTAIN IMPERIAL PIGEON
Ducula badia

L 18½". A large grey pigeon with purplish maroon mantle and broad greyish terminal band on tail. Found in forests up to 7,000 feet (mostly mountains); sometimes in mangroves. Arboreal, and easily overlooked in lofty trees. Probably solitary, or may move in small groups. Call: melodious *click whroom whroom*. Breeds all year. Resident.

CRANES Gruidae

Myanmar has three species of crane, and one is resident.

Cranes are large wading birds with long necks and legs. Their bills are straight and pointed, and equal to or a little longer than the head. They are omnivorous. In flight, they hold their necks outstretched. They nest on ground or in shallow water, building bulky pads of vegetation. Sexes are alike.

95. SARUS CRANE
Grus antigone

L 60". A large grey bird with red head and legs. Found in marshes, grass plains and paddy fields. Sexes similar, and pair for life. Pairs sometimes collect into larger groups. Pairs perform courtship display by wing-spreading, head-lowering, leaping, bowing and trumpeting loudly. Shy. Breeds during the rains. Resident.

96. COMMON CRANE
Grus grus

L 45". A large slate-grey bird with curving white stripe on sides of head and neck and drooping feathers over tail. Dull red nape visible at close range. Found in marshes, swamps and less disturbed cultivations. Gregarious. Walks slowly and gracefully. Shy. Rarely perches on tree. Feeds mainly in mornings and evenings. Call: various honking sounds, *krooh*, *krrooah* and *kurr* etc in flight. Winter visitor, arriving in November and leaving in March, to W, N and E Myanmar.

FINFOOTS Heliornithidae

This family is represented in Myanmar by one species, and it is resident.

Finfoots are aquatic birds, and they superficially resemble grebes. They have long neck, tapered bill and long, pointed wings. Their feet are short with a web round front toes. Plumage is compact and close. They swim low in water with head bobbing back and forth,and can swim partially submerged. When disturbed, they swim ashore and seek safety in nearby undergrowth. They are fine swimmers and divers, and equally strong runners. They live alone or in pairs, and feed on seeds, aquatic insects, crustaceans, snails and frogs.

97. MASKED FINFOOT
Heliopais personata

L 21". An olive brown bird with black face mask and yellow bill; female has whitish patch on centre of throat and foreneck. Found in swamps, flooded forest areas and tidal creeks. Secretive. Often dives under water. Nests in waterside trees or bushes, up to 8 feet above water. Call: series of bubbling sounds. Breeds during the rains. Resident.

95. SARUS CRANE
Grus antigone

94. MOUNTAIN IMPERIAL PIGEON
Ducula badia

97. MASKED FINFOOT
Heliopais personata

96. COMMON CRANE
Grus grus

RAILS, CRAKES, COOTS, Rallidae

Fourteen species of this family occur in Myanmar and eight are resident.

Rails, crakes and coots are marsh waders, capable of swimming. They have laterally compressed bodies and long legs and toes. They have characteristic horizontal body posture, and frequently jerk tail when walking and head when swimming. They fly weakly with legs trailing, but many migrate long distances. They are crepuscular in habits. They feed on seeds, plant shoots, buds etc and also on insects, especially grasshoppers and their larvae. They build nests of reeds or grass in or near water. Sexes are alike in most species.

98. SLATY-BREASTED RAIL
Gallirallus striatus

L 10". A dull olive-brown bird with chestnut crown and hindneck and grey breast; upperparts and belly barred with white. Found in marshes, mangroves and paddy fields. Typically a bird of kaing grass. Shy. Solitary. Flight weak, but a good swimmer and diver. Call: harsh *kerrek*. Breeds all year. Resident, except in W Myanmar.

99. WHITE-BREASTED WATERHEN
Amaurornis phoenicurus

L.13". A blackish bird with white face and underparts. Found in marshes, paddyfields, and mangrove edge; also on canals. Sometimes seen far from water. Often seen clambering about bushes or high up in trees. Not shy, and feeds in open at dusk and dawn. Call: long series of *kwaak, kuk* or *kook*. Breeds from May to July. Common resident.

100. RUDDY-BREASTED CRAKE
Porzana fusca

L 8½". A dark olive-brown bird with reddish-chestnut mask and underparts. Found in freshwater marshes, reedbeds and vegetated wetlands, sometimes in more open wetlands. Very shy, usually seen at dusk and dawn. Call: soft *keek-keek-keek*. Breeds from February to June. Resident, except in Tanintharyi and W Myanmar.

101. WATERCOCK
Gallicrex cinerea

L 17". Male: blackish grey with red bill, red frontal shield and red legs. Female: buff brown with olive-green legs. Male similar to female outside breeding season. Found in marshes, swamps, paddy fields and flooded grazing grounds. Feeds mainly in mornings and evenings. Call: *ogh-ogh-ogh-ogh-ogh-ogh-ogh-ogh-ogh-ogh*. Breeds during the rains. Resident.

102. PURPLE SWAMPHEN
Porphyrio porphyrio

L. 17". A dark purplish blue bird with large red bill and frontal shield. Found in marshes; also in paddy fields. Gregarious. Not shy. Rarely swims, but stalks across floating vegetation. Call: *quinquinkrrkrr*. Breeds from July to September. Resident at low elevations.

103. COMMON MOORHEN
Gallinula chloropus

L 13". A slate-grey bird with yellow-tipped red bill. Found in marshes. Often perches on trees. Jerks tail when nervous. Flies low over water with neck and legs extended. Swims with characteristic bobbing action of head. Dives to escape danger. Call: loud, harsh *prruk*. Breeds during the rains. Resident.

98. SLATY-BREASTED RAIL
Gallirallus striatus

99. WHITE-BREASTED WATERHEN
Amaurornis phoenicurus

100. RUDDY-BREASTED CRAKE
Porzana fusca

101. WATERCOCK
Gallicrex cinerea

102. PURPLE SWAMPHEN
Porphyrio porphyrio

103. COMMON MOORHEN
Gallinula chloropus

104. COMMON COOT
Fulica atra
L 16". A blackish bird with white bill and frontal shield. Found in inland marshes; also on lakes. Swims in shallow water by day with bobbing action of head, often diving for food. Often resorts to fields at dusk and dawn to hunt for insects and snails and also to feed on young crops. Flight weak and laboured. Seldom ventures far from water. Call: loud, harsh *kraw-kraw*. Breeds from April. Resident in Chin State and Mandalay Division; distributed sparsely over rest of the country.

CURLEWS, GODWITS, SANDPIPERS, SNIPE Scolopacidae
This family is represented in Myanmar by thirty-four species, but only one is resident. Members of this family are waders of the shores of lakes, rivers, marshes and seacoasts. They are walking and running birds of small to medium size, often with long legs and long, slender bills. Wings are usually pointed and angular. Plumages often differ in summer, winter and when young, and are often confusing when moulting. Most species are gregarious outside breeding season.

In Myanmar, many species arrive in October and leave by March. Immature and non-breeding adults of many species remain throughout the summer.

105. EURASIAN WOODCOCK
Scolopax rusticola
L 14". A brownish-buff bird with long straight bill; upperparts mottled and underparts barred. Found in open forests and thick cover of marshes and rivers. Crepuscular. Usually solitary. Flight usually rapid and dodging. In flight, looks stout and "neckless" with bill pointing downward at an angle. Utters weak, high-pitched chissick or pissipp interspersed with low, guttural *aurk-aurk-aurk* during roding display. Believed to breed in mountains of N Myanmar. Winter visitor, October to April.

106. PINTAIL SNIPE
Gallinago stenura
L 10". A heavily streaked and mottled bird, distinguished by numerous tail feathers, eight outer pairs being very narrow like pins. Found in marshy areas, paddy fields and grasslands. Feeds at night, resting during the day. Feeds less on worms and more on insects, larvae and molluscs. Call: rasping, rather nasal *squak*. Winter visitor, August to May.

107. COMMON SNIPE
Gallinago gallinago
L 11". A brownish bird with rapid zigzag flight and a harsh call when flushed. Found in dense vegetation in marshy areas and paddy fields. Shy. Sluggish and unwilling to rise during heat of day, but active in mornings and evenings, sometimes flying round in wide circles at a great height. Flight fast and tortuous. Call: dry rasping scaap when flushed. Winter visitor, September to March.

108. EURASIAN CURLEW
Numenius arquata
L 23". A buff brown bird with long curved bill. Found in marshes; also on mudflats and sea coasts. Shy. Usually seen in small parties. Flocks usually fly high in lines or chevrons. Flight strong and rather gull-like with measured beat. Call: loud, musical *cour-li*. Winter visitor, but large numbers of non-breeding birds observed on coastal mudflats at any time in the rains, and a few along the Ayeyarwady River.

104. COMMON COOT
Fulica atra

106. PINTAIL SNIPE
Gallinago stenura

105. EURASIAN WOODCOCK
Scolopax rusticola

107. COMMON SNIPE
Gallinago gallinago

108. EURASIAN CURLEW
Numenius arquata

109. COMMON REDSHANK
Tringa totanus

L 11". A grey brown bird with red legs and base of bill. Found in marshes; also on mudflats and sea coasts. Also frequents paddy fields, tidal creeks and canals. Usually solitary or in pairs. Call: mellow, musical *teu-hu-hu-hu*. Winter visitor, but non-breeding birds observed in hundreds on the coast during the rains.

110. COMMON GREENSHANK
Tringa nebularia

L 14". A grey bird with long, slightly upturned bill and greenish legs. Found in marshes, on mudflats and sea coasts; also on village ponds. Rather shy. Solitary. Flight fast and powerful. Feeds on a variety of small creatures. Call: very loud, ringing, musical *tew tew tew tew* or *chew chew chew chew*. Winter visitor, August to May. Non-breeding individuals seen in June and July.

111. GREEN SANDPIPER
Tringa ochropus

L 9½". A dark greenish brown bird with pale eyebrows. Found in marshes; also frequents streams, ponds, ditches and flood-water. Shy. Solitary, but collects into small parties on migration. Flight rapid. Chases insects with great agility. Call: loud, liquid *tlooi-tlooeet*. Winter visitor, but non-breeding birds observed in any month of the year.

112. COMMON SANDPIPER
Actitis hypoleucos

L 8". A fairly small plain brown bird with white underparts and brownish patch on sides of breast. Found on mudflats, tidal creeks, rivers and ponds. Usually solitary, sometimes seen in small numbers. Incessantly nods head and jerks tail up and down. Normally picks food off surface, rather than probes. Call: shrill, piping *twe-wee wee wee*. Winter visitor, August to May; few individuals remain throughout the year.

PAINTED-SNIPES Rostratulidae

One species of this family occurs in Myanmar, and is resident.

Painted-snipes are plump, tailless birds, and they are superficially similar to true snipe. They live in marshy areas, usually under cover. They are very secretive and mostly nocturnal in habits. They fly a direct, rather slow and steady flight with trailing legs. They can also swim. They feed by probing in soft mud and sweeping bill from side to side in shallow water. Females are larger and more richly coloured, and play dominant roles in sexual matters. Males incubate eggs and rear the young. Both sexes perform spread-wing displays.

113. GREATER PAINTED-SNIPE
Rostratula benghalensis

L 10" (male) 11" (female). A grey brown bird with broad whitish eye-ring and post-ocular stripe. Found in marshes, swamps and paddy fields up to 5,000 feet. Flies well but rises with dangling legs. Feeds on both animal and vegetable life. Female territorial call is a series of 20–80 *kook, oook* or *koh* notes. Breeds in July and August. Resident.

110. COMMON GREENSHANK
Tringa nebularia

109. COMMON REDSHANK
Tringa totanus

111. GREEN SANDPIPER
Tringa ochropus

112. COMMON SANDPIPER
Actitis hypoleucos

113. GREATER PAINTED-SNIPE
Rostratula benghalensis

JACANAS Jacanidae

The jacanas are represented in Myanmar by two species and both are resident.

Jacanas are long-necked tropical marsh birds with long pointed wings and very lengthened toes and claws. They are often seen in scattered flocks. They walk about and run on floating plants in pursuit of insects, and can swim and dive. They fly weakly. They feed on seeds, roots and aquatic invertebrates. Females are larger than males, and one female mates with more than one male, leaving him to care for the eggs and young. Their nest is a floating mass of weeds with a slight depression for eggs. Sexes are alike.

114. PHEASANT-TAILED JACANA
Hydrophasianus chirurgus

L 12" (tail of breeding adult up to 10" more). A blackish brown bird with a black line along side of neck and white underparts. Found in marshes and on lotus ponds. Prefers more open water. Gregarious in winter. Call: nasal mewing *tewn tewn tewn*, also piping *hoo hoo hoo*. Breeds from June to August. Resident at low elevations.

115. BRONZE-WINGED JACANA
Metopidius indicus

L 11". A glossy blackish bird with broad white eyebrow and bronze-olive wing and back. Found in marshes and on lotus ponds. Not shy. Walks on floating vegetation with high-stepping action of feet and accompanying jerk of tail at each step. Call: variety of piping calls and low guttural notes. Breeds during the rains. Resident at low elevations.

THICK-KNEES Burhinidae

Myanmar has three species of thick-knee and all are resident.

Thick-knees are waders with compact bodies and long legs. They have large heads, thick bills and yellow eyes. They are terrestrial and somewhat nocturnal in habits, and feed on mice, lizards, insects, larvae and worms. They nest on the ground.

116. EURASIAN THICK-KNEE
Burhinus oedicnemus

L 16". A sandy brown bird with darker streaks. Found in grass and scrub of open country especially of central Dry Zone; also on sandbanks. Never found in thick forest. Solitary or paired; sometimes in small parties. Often flies low over the ground. Runs furtively with head low and body hunched. Rests on horizontal tarsi. Call: loud *curlivee*. Breeds chiefly in June and July. Resident, except in W and E Myanmar.

117. GREAT THICK-KNEE
Esacus recurvirostris

L 20". A greyish brown bird with black and white facial pattern. Found on rivers and sea coasts. In rains and cold weather, collects into parties of a dozen or twenty birds and haunts grasslands above flood level. Call: wailing *kree kree kree kree kree kree kree kree*. Breeds on sandbanks in hot weather. Resident.

114. PHEASANT-TAILED JACANA
Hydrophasianus chirurgus

115. BRONZE -WINGED JACANA
Metopidius indicus

116. EURASIAN THICK-KNEE
Burhinus oedicnemus

117. GREAT THICK-KNEE
Esacus recurvirostris

IBISBILLS, STILTS, AVOCETS, PLOVERS, LAPWINGS Charadriidae

Seventeen species of this family occur in Myanmar, but only five are resident.

Ibisbills, stilts and avocets are waders with very long legs and long, slender bills. They are gregarious and noisy. They feed on insects, small crustaceans, molluscs, aquatic invertebrates and fish.

Plovers and lapwings are plumpish, thick-necked birds of bare, open ground, usually near water, They are gregarious and often noisy. They run swiftly and fly strongly. They feed almost exclusively on insects, larvae, worms and crustaceans.

118. BLACK-WINGED STILT
Himantopus himantopus

L 15". A black and white bird with reddish legs. Found in marshes; also frequents mudflats, village ponds and flooded paddy fields. Solitary or in small parties. Nervous. Very noisy. Feeds on seeds of water-plants, insects, small molluscs and worms. Many are winter visitors, a few are breeding residents. Call: sharp *kik-kik-kik*. Breeds in June and July.

119. LITTLE RINGED PLOVER
Charadrius dubius

L 7". A brownish bird with a white neck collar. Found on rivers; also in marshes and coastal areas. Prefers sandy and stony margins of rivers and avoids coastal and tidal estuaries. Energetic and lively. Runs and flies well. Call: sharp, plaintive pipe or whistle *pink pink pink*. Breeds during hot weather on sandbanks or shingle. Common resident.

120. RIVER LAPWING
Vanellus duvaucelli

L 12". An olive-brown bird with black crest on upper back and black spur at bend of wing. Found on river bars; also in grasslands, gardens and fallow land when rivers are flooded; also in higher hills locally. Swims well. Call: *dit-dit-to-weet dit-dit-to-weet*. Breeds during hot weather. Eggs laid on sand or shingle. Resident.

121. RED-WATTLED LAPWING
Vanellus indicus

L. 13". An olive-brown bird with black head and upper breast, and white underparts. Found on rivers; also in marshes, rice stubble, cultivations and open forest. Usually seen in pairs or family parties. Call: *did-he-do-it, pity-to-do-it*. Breeds during hot weather. Eggs laid in a scrape on ground. Common resident.

PRATINCOLES, Glareolinae, Glareolidae

Myanmar has two species of pratincole and both are resident.

Pratincoles are small, short-legged birds with short bills, long, pointed wings and forked tails. They are gregarious, and feed on insects by hawking them on the wing, mostly in the evenings. They nest in colonies.

122. ORIENTAL PRATINCOLE
Glareola maldivarum

L 10". A grey brown bird with red base to the bill. Found in open country in rice stubble and marshy areas. Feeds in places many miles from breeding haunts. On ground, runs in short dashes at great speed, feeding on insects. Call: *kyik* or *kyeck, chik-chik* and *chet* etc, usually in flight. Breeds in colonies in burnt rice stubble in hot weather. Resident.

118. BLACK-WINGED STILT
Himantopus himantopus

119. LITTLE RINGEDPLOVER
Charadrius dubius

122. ORIENTAL PRATINCOLE
Glareola maldivarum

120. RIVER LAPWING
Vanellus duvaucelli

121. RED-WATTLED LAPWING
Vanellus indicus

123. SMALL PRATINCOLE
Glareola lactea

L 7". A grey bird, showing bi-coloured wings in flight. Found in marshes and on rivers. Seen in large flocks, skimming over surface of water or running about sandbanks. More active at dusk than during the day. Call: high-pitched *prrip* or *tiririt* in flight. Breeds in April, laying eggs on sandbanks. Resident.

SKIMMERS Rynchopini, Larinae, Laridae

One species of Skimmer occurs in Myanmar, and it is resident.

Skimmers are large, tern-like water birds. They have laterally compressed bill with the lower mandible markedly longer than the upper. They feed in flight by skimming water surface with submerged lower mandible, scooping up fish. They are gregarious. Sexes are alike.

124. INDIAN SKIMMER
Rynchops albicollis

L 17". A black and white bird with orange-red bill. Found on large rivers, lakes and sea coasts. Common on the Ayeyarwaddy and Chindwin rivers. Keeps in small parties. Call: *kap* or *kip* particularly in flight. Breeds on sandbanks in hot weather. Resident, except in Tanintharyi.

GULLS, TERNS Larini, Sternini, Larinae, Laridae

Gulls and terns are represented in Myanmar by eighteen species, of which four are resident.

The Gulls and Terns are excellent fliers, going around in flocks and breeding in colonies. They inhabit sea coasts, lakes and rivers. They usually have different seasonal plumages, with immatures specimens resembling winter adults. Sexes are alike.

The Gulls are large, robust birds with broad wings, rounded tails and slightly hooked bills. They feed on fish and offal. They frequetly sit on the water.

The Terns are slender-bodied birds with pointed bills and forked tails. They feed largely on fish and aquatic animals caught by diving into the water, or picked off the surface; they seldom swim or sit on the water. Some smaller terns hawk insects in flight.

125. BROWN-HEADED GULL
Larus brunnicephalus

L 18". A pale grey gull with white spot on black wing tip; bill and feet, red; head, whitish throughout winter, blackish-brown in summer. Found on rivers and sea coasts. The common gull of the Yangon River. Often flies alongside ships. Feeds largely by scavenging. On Inlay Lake, feeds chiefly on insects. Call: *gek, gek* also *ka-yek, ka-yek*. Winter visitor, September to May.

126. RIVER TERN
Sterna aurantia

L 14". A grey bird with white underparts, yellow bill and red to orange feet; cap, black in summer, white in winter. Found on rivers and sea coasts. Common along the Ayeyarwaddy, the Chindwin and other large rivers and their tributaries, and on Inlay Lake. Feeds on small fish. Call: *kiaah* or *hiaah*. Breeds in April and May, laying eggs on sandbanks, often in company with lapwings, pratincoles, plovers etc. Resident.

123. SMALL PRATINCOLE
Glareola lactea

124. INDIAN SKIMMER
Rynchops albicollis

126. RIVER TERN
Sterna aurantia

125. BROWN-HEADED GULL
Larus brunnicephalus

127. LITTLE TERN
Sterna albifrons

L 9" (outer pairs of tail feathers up to 1" more). A pale grey tern with black-tipped yellow bill and yellow feet, bill blackish, dusky yellow outside breeding season. Found on rivers, lakes and sea coasts. More marine than others in its habits. Solitary or in loose parties. Flight rapid, occasionally hovers. Call: kik or ket particularly in flight. Breeds on sandbanks during hot weather. Resident, except in N Myanmar.

128. BLACK-BELLIED TERN
Sterna acuticauda

L 12" (outer pairs of tail feathers up to 3" more). A dark grey tern with black cap: forecrown and underparts white outside breeding season. Found on rivers, lakes, village ponds and ditches; rarely met on the coast. Feeds almost entirely on fish and small creatures. Call: *krek-kerk*. Breeds from February to May on sandbanks. Resident.

129. WHISKERED TERN
Chlidonias hybridus

L 11". A dark grey tern with black cap, white cheeks and silvery grey upper wing; crown and underparts, whitish with black streak behind eye outside breeding season. Found in marshes and paddy fields; also on lakes and sea coasts. Flies back and forth over water dipping to feed from surface. Feeds on dragonflies and their larvae, water beetles and other aquatic insects. Call: *kersch* and *kek* mainly in flight. Resident and migrant.

OSPREY Pandioninae, Accipitridae

Only one species of this family is suspected of breeding in Myanmar.

The osprey differs from all other hawks chiefly anatomically; the claws are relatively powerfully hooked, and the outer toe is a turning toe. In flight, long narrow wings are held angled. It feeds on fish which it catches by plunge-diving.

130. OSPREY
Pandion haliaetus

L 20–23". A blackish brown bird with white head and neck, and broad blackish eye-line; underparts, white with dusky breast-band. Found on rivers, lakes and sea coasts. Single birds observed in June, July and August in Myitkyina, Pyin-Oo-Lwin and Yangon. In winter, seen all over the country. Call: *piu piu piu piu*.

KITES, HAWKS, EAGLES, VULTURES Accipitrinae, Accipitridae

Fifty species of this group occur in Myanmar, and twenty-six are resident.

The raptors are characterised by their sharp, hooked bills, strong feet and sharp claws. Plumages are highly variable. Sexes are generally alike, but females are usually larger than males. Most species are predatory, but some are scavengers. Most species build untidy stick nests.

Vultures are huge birds with naked head and neck. At rest, the hunched-up high-shouldered posture is characteristic. In flight, when soaring for hours on almost motionless wings, they look majestic.

Vultures rarely take prey alive. They spend much of their time circling high up in the sky on the look-out for food. When food (acarcases) is sighted, they settle on the ground and walk clumsily or hop ungainly towards it. Having gorged their fill, they sit on the ground or rise with difficulty to a nearby tree before flying off to their favourite tree for rest.

Vultures build nests with sticks in high trees and use them year after year. Only one egg is laid.

127. LITTLE TERN
Sterna albifrons

128. BLACK-BELLIED TERN
Sterna acuticauda

129. WHISKERED TERN
Chlidonias hybridus

130. OSPREY
Pandion haliaetus

131. BLACK BAZA
Aviceda leuphotes

L 13". A black bird with long crest, white breast band and brown-barred white abdomen. Found in open forests, secondary growth and villages up to 4,000 feet. Gregarious, parties of seven to twelve birds observed. Usually active in mornings and evenings. Feeds on insects. Call: *chi-aah, tchi'euuah* or *tcheeoua*. Breeds from March to May. Resident.

132. ORIENTAL HONEY-BUZZARD
Pernis ptilorhyncus

L 20". A polymorphic species, usually with dark brown upper parts and almost white to dark brown underparts; streaked or barred or without markings. Found in open wooded country and cultivated fields; often near towns. Feeds mainly on bees and honey; also on reptiles including snakes and small mammals. Call: *wheeew*. Breeds from March to May. Resident and migrant.

133. BLACK-SHOULDERED KITE
Elanus caeruleus

L 13". An ashy white kite with black shoulder patch, pure white underparts and long pointed wings. Found in paddy plains; also frequents well-wooded country. Flight, slow and deliberate, and often hovers. Solitary or paired. Active in mornings and evenings, resting in isolated trees during heat of the day. Feeds on mice, large insects etc. Call: soft, piping *pii-uu* or *pieu* particularly when displaying. Breeds from January to April. Resident up to 5,000 feet, except in Tanintharyi.

134. BLACK KITE
Milvus migrans

L 26". A dark brown bird with forked tail. Found in open and coastal areas; also frequents rivers, harbours and cities up to 5,000 feet. A common breeding bird in the plains, but disappears at the break of the rains. Feeds largely on offal. Call: pee-errr or ewe-wirrrrr. Breeds from October to April. Resident, mostly at low elevations.

135. BRAHMANY KITE
Haliastur indus

L 18". A bright chestnut bird with white head and breast. Found in coastal areas and mangroves and on larger rivers and around edges of towns. Normally a scavenger, especially near fishing villages. Call: *tsss, herheh heh heh heh heh*. Breeds from January to March. Builds nest in solitary tree growing in cultivations or beside a water body. Resident up to 6,000 feet, but mostly in lowlands.

136. WHITE-BELLIED SEA EAGLE
Haliaeetus leucogaster

L 28". An ashy-brown bird with pure white head, neck and underparts. Found in coastal areas, ascending larger rivers for 60 miles or so. Very confiding. Feeds mainly on fish and water snakes. Call: loud honking *kank kank kank* or *blank blank blank blank*, shorter, quicker *ken ken ken ken* and *kakakaa*. Breeds from October to February. Builds nest in high trees. Common resident along coasts.

132. ORIENTAL HONEY-BUZZARD
Pernis ptilorhyncus

135. BRAHMANY KITE
Haliastur indus

131. BLACK BAZA
Aviceda leuphotes

134. BLACK KITE
Milvus migrans

133. BLACK-SHOULDERED KITE
Elanus caeruleus

136. WHITE-BELLIED SEA EAGLE
Haliaeetus leucogaster

137. PALLAS'S FISH EAGLE
Haliaeetus leucoryphus
L 32". A dark brown bird with tawny head, neck, upper back, throat and upper breast; tail, white with black tip. Found on large rivers, lakes and sometimes coasts. Primarily a freshwater fisher and common fishing eagle of the Ayeyarwaddy River. Also preys on birds and reptiles and eats carrion. Call: *kha kha kha kha, gho gho gho gho, gao gao gao gao*. Breeds from November to February. Resident up to 9,000 feet.

138. WHITE-RUMPED VULTURE
Gyps bengalensis
L 35". A huge blackish bird with white lower back and rump. Found in open and partly wooded country up to 4,500 feet. The commonest vulture in the plains, making casual visits to higher hills. Often silent, but gives occasional grunts, croaks, hisses and squeals at nest-sités, roosts and when feeding. Breeds from September to December. Resident.

139. LONG-BILLED VULTURE
Gyps indicus
L 35". A huge sandy-brown bird with dark head and neck and yellow bill. Found in open and partly wooded country. Less common than White-rumped Vulture. Often silent, but gives occasional hissing and cackling sounds. Breeds in December and January. Resident, except in N Myanmar. Common in SW Myanmar.

140. RED-HEADED VULTURE
Sarcogyps calvus
L 32". A huge blackish bird with red naked head and feet. Found in open and partly wooded country up to 5,000 feet. Less gregarious than other vultures, sometimes solitary. Flight effortless. Often silent, but gives occasional squeaks, hisses and grunts. Breeds from October to January. Resident.

141. CRESTED SERPENT EAGLE
Spilornis cheela
L 26–28". A dark brown bird with partially erectile crest lying on nape. Found in forests and well-wooded country up to 5,000 feet. Can fly very high, even out of sight. Feeds mainly on snakes, also on frogs, lizards, insects and birds. Rather vocal, utters on the wing a plaintive whistling call of several notes, *kuk kuk kuk kuk-queear queear queear queear*. Breeds from February to April. Builds nest in trees. Common resident at all elevations.

142. PIED HARRIER
Circus melanoleucos
L 17–18". Male: black and white. Female: dark brown above and pale fulvous-rufous below. Found in marshes, paddy fields and grass plains. Flight, slow and flapping, a few feet above ground when hunting. Feeds on small mammals. Usually silent, but occasionally utters a rapid *wek-wek-wek*. Breeds from April to June. Resident in N Myanmar; migrant over rest of the country, from September to April.

143. CRESTED GOSHAWK
Accipiter trivirgatus
L 16". A dark brown bird with short crest. Found in forest and secondary growth in foothills and higher hills up to 6,000 feet. Sedentary. Often frequents forest clearings. Feeds on birds, small mammals, reptiles and large insects. Breeds from December to September. Resident, except in SW Myanmar.

137. PALLAS'S FISH EAGLE
Haliaeetus leucoryphus

138. WHITE-RUMPED VULTURE
Gyps bengalensis

139. LONG-BILLED VULTURE
Gyps indicus

140. RED-HEADED VULTURE
Sarcogyps calvus

141. CRESTED SERPENT EAGLE
Spilornis cheela

143. CRESTED GOSHAWK
Accipiter trivirgatus

♂

♀

142. PIED HARRIER
Circus melanoleucos

144. SHIKRA
Accipiter badius
L 12–14". A bluish grey bird, brownish grey in females. Found in open country with wooded areas, often near towns and villages up to 5,000 feet. Frequents streams and glades in teak forests. Hides in leafy trees and launches surprise attacks on prey. In forest fires, seen hawking insects, also reptiles. Call: *titu-titu* and *theeya-theeya*. Breeds in March and Apirl. Common resident, mostly at low elevations.

145. WHITE-EYED BUZZARD
Butastur teesa
L 16". A dark brown bird with white eyes and white nape-patch. Found in dry open country. Often seen sitting sluggishly on telephone posts, trees or shrubs. Remarkably fearless of man. Feeds on grasshoppers and other insects which it picks up on the ground. Call: *pit-weeer pit-weeer pit-weeer*. Breeds from February to May. Resident, except in N and E Myanmar.

146. RUFOUS-WINGED BUZZARD
Butastur liventer
L 16". A dull brownish bird with white thighs and black-tipped yellow bill. Found in thin forests and open wooded areas, often near lakes or rivers up to 5,000 feet. Feeds mainly on reptiles. Call: *pit-piu*. Breeds in March and April. Resident.

147. CHANGEABLE HAWK EAGLE
Spizaetus cirrhatus
L 27". A polymorphic species; dark brown or blackish brown. Found in forests, open wooded areas and secondary growth in foothills and higher hills up to 7,000 feet. Feeds on doves, domestic poultry, waterfowls etc. Usually nests near top of large tree. Call: *yeep-yip yip yip, yeep-yip yip yip*. Breeds from November to May. Resident.

FALCONS Falconidae
Myanmar has ten species of falcon, and six are resident.

Falcons are slim, powerful birds with long pointed wings, long, slightly tapered tails and rapid pigeon-like flight, occasionally broken by long glides. When perched, head appears large, and long wings reach to end of tail. When soaring, some species fan their wings, producing more rounded appearance. Females are larger than males. They feed primarily on insects and birds, often caught in flight. Falconets nest on ledges or take over the deserted nests of other birds.

148. COLLARED FALCONET
Microhierax caerulescens
L 7½". A blackish bird with black-crowned white head and broad black line through the eye; underparts, mainly white. Found in open forest and forest edge up to 6,000 feet: partial to clearings, fields, taungyas and other open spaces surrounded by forest. Common in teak forests of Bago Yoma. Often seen in pairs or small groups. Feeds on grasshoppers, beetles, small birds etc. Call: *kli kli kli* or *killi killi killi*. Breeds from February to May. Common resident.

145. WHITE -EYED BUZZARD
Butastur teesa

144. SHIKRA
Accipiter badius

146. RUFOUS-WINGED BUZZARD
Butastur liventer

Blackish Phase

Light Phase

147. CHANGABLE HAWK EAGLE
Spizaetus cirrhatus

148. COLLARED FALCONET
Microhierax caerulescens

149. COMMON KESTREL
Falco tinnunculus

L 13½". A rufous brown bird with longer tail than other falcons; head and tail, grey in male. Found in open country in the plains and higher hills up to 6,000 feet. Usually solitary. Hovers in pursuit of mice, voles, insects etc. Perches on trees, telegraph poles, rocks etc. Believed to breed in Rakhine and Chin Hills. Call: *keee keee keee*. Winter visitor, October to April.

150. PEREGRINE FALCON
Falco peregrinus

L 15–19". A slate-grey bird with broad blackish moustache and white cheek patch. Found in open country in paddy fields and coastal areas. Crepuscular. Feeds on birds, bats and occasionally carrion. Builds nest on cliff or river bank. Breeds from March to May. Resident (subspecies *peregrinator*), winter visitor (subspecies *japonensis*), November to early April.

GREBES Podicipedidae

The grebes are represented in Myanmar by three species, but only one is resident.

Grebes are duck-like, aquatic birds with short, rounded wings and pointed bill. They feed on small fish, aquatic insects, crustaceans and pieces of plant, and nest on floating vegetation. Sexes are alike.

151. LITTLE GREBE
Tachybaptus ruficollis

L 10". A dark brown bird with a tailless appearance. Found on ponds, lakes and canals; also in marshes. Often seen in large flocks on open water outside breeding season. Can swim partially submerged. Prefers to dive rather than take flight when alarmed. Territorial call is a shrill whinnying trill. Breeds during the rains. Resident.

DARTERS, Anhingidae

One species of darter occurs in Myanmar, and it is resident.

Darters are similar to cormorants, but have more slender, snake-like necks and narrower, pointed bills and longer, fan-shaped tails. They live on rivers, lakes and in marshes and build nests on nearby trees. Sexes are alike.

152. DARTER
Anhinga melanogaster

L 36". A black bird with long, snake-like neck; head and throat, light brown; chin, white; scapulars and shoulders, silver grey. A freshwater bird found in flocks, often in company with little cormorants, on lakes and in marshes. Swims very low in water, often with only head and neck above surface. Frequently dives while swimming, appearing some distance away. Sometimes soars. Tail spread like a fan in flight. Usually silent. Breeds during the rains. Resident.

CORMORANTS Phalacrocoracidae

Myanmar has three species of Cormorant and all are resident.

Cormorants are large, aquatic birds with webbed feet. Most are black. They have a long bill which ends in a sharp hook, a long neck and rather wedge-shaped tail. When swimming on surface, bill is often held tilted slightly upwards. They sometimes swim with only head above surface. When diving, they can reach quite far down. They often perch with outstretched wings. Flight is direct and strong with outstretched neck. They feed on fish and eels, and roost and nest in colonies in trees. Sexes are alike.

149. COMMON KESTREL
Falco tinnunculus

150. PEREGRINE FALCON
Falco peregrinus

151. LITTLE GREBE
Tachybaptus ruficollis

152. DARTER
Anhinga melanogaster

153. LITTLE CORMORANT
Phalacrocorax niger

L 20". A black bird with short bill; neck, comparatively short. Found in freshwater marshes; also on ponds, lakes and rivers, occasionally on coast. Seen singly or in large flocks. Breeds from May to September, in company with darters and egrets. Resident.

154. GREAT CORMORANT
Phalacrocorax carbo

L 32". A blackish bird with long heavy bill and bronze sheen on back. Found on lakes and rivers; also in marshes. A freshwater bird often seen in large flocks. Swims low with head erect. Dips into water when alarmed with only head and neck above surface. When at rest, sits on shore or perches on rocks or trees with outspread wings. Flight direct and fairly swift. Usually silent. Breeds from October to January. Reported as breeding in the Sittaung valley. Resident in S Myanmar.

HERONS, EGRETS, BITTERNS Ardeidae

Twenty-one species of this family occur in Myanmar, and fourteen are resident.

Herons, egrets, and bitterns are long-necked, long-legged wading birds with pointed bills. They have broad, rounded wings and a slow wing-beat. They feed on small fish, frogs, crabs and insects, and nest in colonies in trees. Their calls are loud croaks and squawks. Some species are crepuscular and /or nocturnal. Sexes are alike or nearly so.

155. LITTLE EGRET
Egretta garzetta

L 24". A snow-white egret with long drooping crest: bill. legs and feet, black. Found in paddy fields from break of rains till harvest; marshes, lakes, streams and mangroves at other times. Gregarious. Call: *kyarrk* or *aaahk* when flushed. Breeds during the rains. Common resident at low elevations.

156. GREY HERON
Ardea cinerea

L 40". A light grey heron with white head and neck, and black streaks on neck. Found in swamps, mangroves, and paddy fields; also on lakes, rivers and mudflats. Largely crepuscular. Typically solitary, but flocks of up to twenty birds sometimes seen. Perches freely on trees. Often stands erect and motionless on ground with neck sunk between shoulders. Call: *krahnk* in flight. Breeds from March to September. Resident, except in W Myanmar where they are migrants.

157. PURPLE HERON
Ardea purpurea

L 26". A greyish bird with rufous neck and underparts. Found in swamps and mangroves throughout the plains; also on lakes. Crepuscular and secretive. Solitary outside breeding season. Quietly stalks prey with slow deliberate movements. Call: *krahnk* in flight. Breeds from July to September. Resident in lowlands.

153. LITTLE CORMORANT
Phalacrocorax niger

154. GREAT CORMORANT
Phalacrocorax carbo

155. LITTLE EGRET
Egretta garzetta

156. GREY HERON
Ardea cinerea

157. PURPLE HERON
Ardea purpurea

Birds of Myanmar

158. GREAT EGRET
Casmerodius albus

L 35". A white egret with blackish legs and yellow-based dusky bill; bill, all yellow outside breeding season. Found in paddy fields, marshes and mangroves; also on lakes and rivers. Familiar on paddy plains during the rains. Solitary outside breeding season. Call: various guttural calls at breeding colonies. Breeds during the rains. Common resident at low elevations.

159. CATTLE EGRET
Bubulcus ibis

L 20". A white egret with yellow bill; head, neck and back, rufous in breeding season. Found in paddy fields, pastures and marshes. Keeps in flocks at all seasons. Seen constantly in company with grazing cattle, often perching on their backs. Feeds chiefly on grasshoppers and flies, sometimes on small fish and aquatic insects. Call: *ruk* or *RIK-rak* in flight. Breeds from April to July. Resident at low elevations.

160. INDIAN POND HERON
Ardeola grayii

L 18". A dingy-coloured bird, usually seen standing montionless on the mud or in water. Found on village ponds and in marshes, paddy fields and mangroves. Solitary, but sometimes seen in twos. Collects in hundreds along the coast on huge expanses of grass-covered mud. Call: urrh urrh urrh in flight. Breeds during the rains. Common resident at low elevations.

161. LITTLE HERON
Butorides striatus

L 18". A slate-grey heron with black crown and long crest. Found on lakes, streams and mudflats and in mangroves. Crepuscular. Solitary and secretive when not breeding. Call: *skeow, k-yow* or *k-yek* when flushed. Breeds from March to October. Crepuscular during breeding season. Common resident up to 3,000 feet.

162. BLACK-CROWNED NIGHT HERON
Nycticorax nycticorax

L 24". A grey bird with black cap and mantle and long drooping white crest. Found in marshes and mangroves. Nocturnal, shy and secretive. Gregarious. Roosts in colones in thickly foliaged tree at dawn. Call: throaty *kwok* when going from daytime roost to feeding grounds at dusk. Breeds from April to September, often in pure colonies. Resident at low elevations.

163. CINNAMON BITTERN
Ixobrychus cinnamomeus

L 15". Males are cinnamon-chestnut; females, chestnut-brown. Found in paddy fields, marshes, reeds and grasses up to 6,000 feet. Secretive and rarely seen. Solitary. Neither shy nor crepuscular in breeding season. Call: *ikh* or *ikh-ikh* in flight. Breeds during the rains. Common resident.

164. BLACK BITTERN
Dupetor flavicollis

L 24". A blackish bird with large buff yellow patch on sides of neck and buff streaks from chin to upper breast. Found in reeds, swamps, paddy fields and mangroves; also on forest streams. Secretive and keeps to dense vegetation. Nocturnal and usually solitary. Breeds from June to September in colonies with egrets. Resident at low elevations.

158. GREAT EGRET
Casmerodius albus

Non-breeding

159. CATTLE EGRET
Bubulcus ibis

Breeding

160. INDIAN POND HERON
Ardeola grayii

161. LITTLE HERON
Butorides striatus

162. BLACK-CROWNED NIGHT HERON
Nycticorax nycticorax

163. CINNAMON BITTERN
Ixobrychus cinnamomeus

164. BLACK BITTERN
Dupetor flavicollis

IBISES, SPOONBILLS Threskiornithidae

This family is represented in Myanmar by five species, of which three are resident.

Ibises and spoonbills are large wading birds. They feed on fish, crabs and small aquatic animals. They fly with necks and legs extended, and often soar. They are gregarious, and nest in colonies with other species in trees.

Ibises have long, thin decurved bills, and spoonbills have flattend bills with spatulate tip.

165. GLOSSY IBIS
Plegadis falcinellus

L 25". A blackish bird with glossy green upper parts; head and neck, brown with white streaks in non-breeding plumage and chestnut-maroon in breeding plumage. Found in swamps and open forest; also on lakes. Perches freely on trees. May give a low harsh graa and subdued grunting sounds in flight. Breeds in May in colonies. Resident at low elevations, except in N Myanmar.

166. BLACK-HEADED IBIS
Threskiornis melanocephalus

L 30". A white bird with black bill, head and neck. Found in marshes and paddy fields; also on lakes and sea coast. Gregarious. Perches freely on trees. Widespread except in N Myanmar. Abundant along coastal areas of Rakhine, Ayeyarwaddy Division and Tanintharyi. Non-breeding winter visitor.

167. WHITE-SHOULDERED IBIS
Pseudibis davisoni

L 30". A dark brown bird with glossy black wings and tail, white patch on inner lesser wing coverts showing in flight. Found in marshes and along muddy banks of streams. Solitary or in pairs, often in small family parties. Very shy. Utters a weird and characteristic cry when rising from the ground. Breeds in February and March. Resident in W, C and S Myanmar.

168. EURASIAN SPOONBILL
Platalea leucorodia

L 33". A tall white bird with long flat spatulate bill; bill, legs and feet, black; facial skin, yellow; has an orange-tawny patch at base of neck. Found on mudflats and swamps. Flight regular and slow, gliding and soaring on extended wings. Feeds by immersing bill in water and sweeping it side to side. A rare winter visitor to SW and S Myanmar.

PELICANS Pelecanidae

Two species of Pelican occur in Myanmar. Breeding colonies of the Spot-billed pelican were reported in the Sittaung valley about 1935. The Great White Pelican, Pelecanus onocrotalus, is a winter visitor to Myanmar.

Pelicans are large aquatic birds with distinctive pouched bills and webbed feet. They are gregarious, and often fish in a coordinated effort. They fly in lines and often soar with heads and curved necks resting on shoulders. They nest in trees. Sexes are alike.

165. GLOSSY IBIS
Plegadis falcinellus

166. BLACK-HEADED IBIS
Threskiornis melanocephalus

167. WHITE-SHOULDERED IBIS
Pseudibis davisoni

168. EURASIAN SPOONBILL
Platalea leucorodia

169. SPOT-BILLED PELICAN
Pelecanus philippensis
L 55". A silvery-grey bird with whitish spectacle around eye; lower back and under-parts, pinkish in breeding plumage. Found on large lakes, rivers and sea coast. Walks clumsily on land. Also perches on trees. Feeds largely on fish. Nests in colonies. Breeds from July to October/November.

STORKS Ciconiidae
The storks are represented in Myanmar by seven species, of which five are resident.

Storks are large wading birds with long legs, long necks and long, massive bills. They are gregarious, and feed on fish, frogs, reptiles and a variety of small animals, both aquatic and terrestrial. They often soar. They build nests in trees and on cliffs. Sexes are alike.

170. PAINTED STORK
Mycteria leucocephala
L 40". A white stork with orange-yellow bill and black and white wings; facial skin, red in breeding season. Found on coastal mudflats; frequents flooded marshes and paddy fields; also lakes. Feeds mainly on fish which it catches by forming a line with others of its species. Nests colonially with other birds. Breeds in tall trees from November to May. Resident at low elevations in C and S Myanmar.

171. ASIAN OPENBILL
Anastomus oscitans
L 32". A white stork with black flight feathers and a curious bill which has a gap be-tween the mandibles. Found on rivers and lakes; also in marshes and paddy fields at low elevations. Has an energetic and sustained flight. Feeds chiefly on freshwater mol-luscs which it crushes before swallowing: also eats crabs, fish, reptiles and large insects. Probably resident.

172. WOOLLY-NECKED STORK
Ciconia episcopus
L 36". A large black stork with white neck. Found on lakes and rivers; also in marshes and paddy fields. Seen in pairs along streams in deep forests. Often associates with other storks and soars at great heights. Feeds on reptiles, frogs, fish etc. Breeds from March to October. Resident at low elevations.

173. BLACK-NECKED STORK
Ephippiorhynchus asiaticus
L 52". A huge stork with black head, neck and tail. Eye, red in male, yellow in female. Found on rivers and lakes; also in swamps. Keeps in pairs or family parties. Rests on tops of trees. On ground, rests with the tarsi flat on ground. Breeds from December to February. Resident in N, C, S and E Myanmar.

174. LESSER ADJUTANT
Leptoptilos javanicus
L 45". A blackish stork with yellowish neck; lacks neck ruff and pouch. Found chiefly in mangroves; also in marshes and paddy fields and on lakes. Occasionally seen in the plains throughout the country; common in Rakhine in winter. Solitary. Not a carrion eater. Feeds mainly on live reptiles, fish, shellfish etc. Breeds from October to June. Resident at low elevations in Tanintharyi.

169. SPOT-BILLED PELICAN
Pelecanus philippensis

170. PAINTED STORK
Mycteria leucocephala

171. ASIAN OPENBILL
Anastomus oscitans

172. WOOLLY-NECKED STROK
Ciconia episcopus

173. BLACK-NECKED STORK
Ephippiorhynchus asiaticus

174. LESSER ADJUTANT
Leptoptilos javanicus

175. GREATER ADJUTANT
Leptoptilos dubius

L 57". A huge stork with naked yellowish head and neck, white neck ruff and pale grey band on wings; yellow pouch hangs from neck. Head and neck, reddish in breeding season. Found in open plains in marshes and paddy fields; also on lakes. Solitary or paired. Has a powerful, majestic and sustained flight. Omnivorous, including carrion. Breeds in November and December. Widespread, but uncommon in most parts of the country during rains. Resident at low elevations in Tanintharyi.

PITTAS Pittidae

Ten species of pitta occur in Myanmar, and eight are resident.

Pittas are terrestrial forest birds with plump bodies, stout bills and long legs. Many are brilliantly coloured. They stay in undergrowth and run when disturbed. They feed on insects, grubs, worms and snails. They build nests either on ground or in understorey trees.

176. RUSTY-NAPED PITTA
Pitta oatesi

L 10". A tawny-rufous bird with greenish wings and back; female has slight rufous tinge on wings and back. Found in forests and secondary growth at 3,000–6,000 feet. Call: a melodious bong-bong. Breeds from December to September. Resident, except in W and C Myanmar.

177. BLUE PITTA
Pitta cyanea

L 9½". Male: blue upper parts and pale blue underparts, barred and spotted with black. Female: duller overall and browner above. Found in forests and secondary growth of the plains and foothills. Feeds chiefly on ants and termites. Call: a *choooo-wit*. Breeds from April to September. Resident, except in N and C Myanmar.

178. HOODED PITTA
Pitta sordida

L 7½". A green pitta with black hood and dark brown crown. Sexes alike. Found in evergreen forests, scrub-jungle and grasslands mainly of the foothills up to 3,000 feet. Shy. Call: *whep-whep* or *whew-whew*. Breeds from May to October. Resident and migrant.

179. BLUE-WINGED PITTA
Pitta moluccensis

L 8". A bluish bird with rufous-buff breast and belly. Sexes alike. Found in mangroves, forests and scrub up to 2,000 feet. A typical bird of teak forests of Bago Yoma during the rains. Call: *taew-laew taew-laew*. Breeds from April to August. Resident, except in C and N Myanmar.

BROADBILLS Eurylaimidae

Myanmar has seven species of broadbill and all are resident.

Broadbills are arboreal forest birds with large heads and broad bills. They are brightly coloured. They feed mostly on insects and small animals and also occasionally take fruits. They live in flocks and are active at dawn and dusk. They build hanging nests over forest streams.

175. GREATER ADJUTANT
Leptoptilos dubius

176. RUSTY-NAPED PITTA
Pitta oatesi

177. BLUE PITTA
Pitta cyanea

178. HOODED PITTA
Pitta sordida

179. BLUE-WINGED PITTA
Pitta moluccensis

180. LONG-TAILED BROADBILL
Psarisomus dalhousiae
L 11". A green bird with black and yellow head and blue tail. Found in evergreen forests up to 5,500 feet. Continuously on the move, jerking tail up and down and searching the leaves for insects. Call: piercing *tseeay* or *pseew*. Breeds from April to June. Resident.

181. SILVER-BREASTED BROADBILL
Serilophus lunatus
L 7". An ash-brown bird with black supercillium; female has a gorget of silvery white feathers across upper breast. Found in forests and bamboo groves up to 6,000 feet (usually mountains). Keeps in small, slow-moving parties. Confiding and fearless. Call: melancholy *ki-uu* or *pee-uu*. Breeds from March to July. Resident.

FAIRY BLUEBIRDS, LEAFBIRDS Irenidae
This family is represented in Myanmar by six species, and all are resident.

Fairy bluebirds are blue and black in colour, and are mostly found in small flocks near fruiting trees. They feed exclusively on fruits.

Leafbirds are small, arboreal birds, moving about in small, noisy parties in mixed feeding flocks. They favour forest canopy and feed on insects, fruits and nectar.

182. ASIAN FAIRY BLUEBIRD
Irena puella
L 10". A blue and black bird with red eyes. Found in moist and evergreen forests of foothills, often ascending to 5,000 feet. Usually in loose flocks. Keeps to treetops. Often stands immobile. Especially fond of figs. Habitually comes down to streams in middle of the day to drink and bathe. Song mellow and loud. Breeds from March to May. Common resident.

183. BLUE-WINGED LEAFBIRD
Chloropsis cochinchinensis
L 7". A green bird with bright blue patches on wings and tail; female lacks black throat patch of male. Found in forests of the plains and foothills up to 4,000 feet. Keeps in small parties, often associating with mixed species feeding flocks. Song consists of various musical liquid notes, pli-pli, chu-chu, chi-chi-pli-i. Breeds from April to August. Resident.

184. GOLDEN-FRONTED LEAFBIRD
Chloropsis aurifrons
L 7½". A green bird with bright orange forehead and blue throat. Found in deciduous and open forests of the plains and foothills, ascending to 4,000 feet. A remarkable mimic, imitating the calls of many other species. Partial to flowering letpan trees. Song is complex, squeaky and scratchy but quite melodious. Breeds from May to August. Common resident.

185. ORANGE-BELLIED LEAFBIRD
Chloropsis hardwickii
L 7½". A green bird with yellow orange belly and under tail coverts; male has black face, throat and upper breast. Young birds acquire adult plumage at one year of age. Found in open forests at 2,000–7,000 feet, particularly along watercourses. Song full and melodious. Breeds from May to August. Resident.

180. LONG -TAILED BROADBILL
Psarisomus dalhousiae

181. SILVER-BREASTED BROADBILL
Serilophus lunatus

♀

♂

♀

182. ASIAN FAIRY BLUEBIRD
Irena puella

♂

♀

183. BLUE-WINGED LEAFBIRD
Chloropsis cochinchinensis

♂

♀

♂

184. GOLDEN-FRONTED LEAFBIRD
Chloropsis aurifrons

185. ORANGE-BELLIED LEAFBIRD
Chloropsis hardwickii

SHRIKES Laniidae

Five species of Shrike occur in Myanmar and two are resident.

Shrikes are predatory passerine birds with strong hooked bills. They have large heads and long tails. They live in open country and prey on insects, lizards, frogs, small rodents and sometimes small birds. They slowly sway their tails when perched. They are solitary and somewhat territorial. They build nests in bushes or trees.

186. BROWN SHRIKE
Lanius cristatus

L 7½". A grey brown bird with white eyebrows and broad black band through the eye. Found in the plains in open country, secondary growth and gardens up to 7,000 feet from about September to May. Often perches on telephone wires. Song consists of a rich and varied chattering. Winter visitor.

187. BURMESE SHRIKE
Lanius collurioides

L 8". A blackish bird with black mask and chestnut upper parts. Found in scrub and cultivation up to 6,000 feet. Common in the plains of C Myanmar from June to March. Song is subdued, quiet, rapid and scratchy, including much repetition and varied mimicry. Breeds in mountains of W, N and E Myanmar from March to June. Some pairs remain in the plains to breed. Resident.

188. LONG-TAILED SHRIKE
Lanius schach

L 10". A sandy-rufous bird with black head and long blackish tail. Found in open country and scrub up to 7,000 feet. Not shy and perches conspicuously on bushes, telephone wires etc. Supposed to swear and chatter at passers-by in their breeding quarters. Song consists of subdued, scratchy warbling notes, incorporating mimicry. Breeds from April to July. Resident in N, C and E Myanmar.

CROWS, JAYS, MAGPIES Corvini, Corvinae, Corvidae

Crows and their allies are represented in Myanmar by seventeen species and sixteen are resident.

Members of this group are mostly large and stocky birds with strong bills, legs and feet. They are typically gregarious and noisy. They are more or less omnivorous. Sexes are alike.

Crows are black in colour; they are bold and aggressive, and frequent open country, usually around human settlements. Jays, magpies and treepies are mostly brightly coloured birds; they are shy and favour forested areas.

189. EURASIAN JAY
Garrulus glandarius

L 13". A pinkish-brown bird with pale blue eyes, black crown and malar patch and white throat and sides of head. Found in forests up to 7,000 feet; partial to indaing forests in the plains and oak and pine forests in higher hills. Usually in pairs or small noisy parties. Keeps to treetops, but often seen hopping on the ground in search of food. Flight heavy. Call: loud and very harsh *skaak-skaak*, prolonged high-pitched mewing *whee-chu whee-chu*. Breeds from March to May. Resident.

188. LONG-TAILED SHRIKE
Lanius schach

186. BROWN SHRIKE
Lanius cristatus

187. BURMESE SHRIKE
Lanius collurioides

189. EURASIAN JAY
Garrulus glandarius

190. RED-BILLED BLUE MAGPIE
Urocissa erythrorhyncha
L 26" (including 19" tail). A blue bird with whitish underparts, black head and throat and bright red bill. Found in forests of the plains and foothills, ascending to 5,000 feet. Arboreal. Frequents undergrowth and lower canopy. Flight fast and undulating. Often feeds on ground, hopping with tail held high. Call: *chweh chweh chweh chweh* or chwit-*wit-wit*. Breeds from March to May. Resident, except in Tanintharyi.

191. COMMON GREEN MAGPIE
Cissa chinensis
L 15" (8" tail inclusive). A green bird with black mask and chestnut-red wings. Plumage changes to blue in captivity, in ill-health and after death. Found in forests and secondary growth. Shy. Solitary or in small parties, often associating with mixed species feeding flocks. Call: loud, shrill *kwee*p. Breeds from March to July. Resident.

192. RUFOUS TREEPIE
Dendrocitta vagabunda
L 17" (including 9" tail). A rufous-brown bird with black head and throat. Found in forests and secondary growth of foothills, locally ascending to 7,000 feet. A typical bird of teak forests. Arboreal and frequents treetops and undergrowth, usually in pairs, often in small parties. Call: *koku-lii* or *koku-wli*. Breeds from February to May. Resident.

193. RACKET-TAILED TREEPIE
Crypsirina temia
L 13" including 8" tail. A black bird with long, broad-ended tail and blue eyes. Found in open country, secondary growth, scrub and cultivations up to 3,000 feet. Strictly arboreal, rarely visiting the ground. Hides inside foliage, and never perches in exposed position, Solitary or paired. Call: short, ringing *chu*, harsh *charaak-chraak*. Breeds from May to July. Common resident in S and E Myanmar and Tanintharyi.

194. HOODED TREEPIE
Crypsirina cucullata
L 12" (including 7"–8" tail). An endemic resident found below 3,000 feet in Dry Zone of C Myanmar, extending to Upper Chindwin and Myitkyina District in the north and to Ayeyarwaddy and Sittaung valleys in the south, down to Yangon. Prefers drier forests, and partial to dense regrowth on edges of cultivations. Call: purring *drrrriiiik*. Breeds from May to July.

195. HOUSE CROW
Corvus splendens
L 17". A black bird with greyish neck, breast and upper back. Found in open plains and cities up to 5,000 feet; also in mangroves. Common in towns and villages; not found in forests. Roosts communally. Call: high-pitched rasping *ka* or down-turning *kow*, low-pitched *kowk*. Breeds in March and April. Common resident.

196. LARGE-BILLED CROW
Corvus macrorhynchos
L 20". An entirely black bird with massive bill. Found in open country, secondary growth, mangroves, and cities up to 7,000 feet. Gregarious and roosts communally. Call: harsh, throaty *khaa* or *kwaa*, also high-pitched *awa, awa, awa*. Breeds from January to April. Common resident.

191. COMMON GREEN MAGPIE
Cissa chinensis

193. RACKET-TAILED TREEPIE
Crypsirina temia

190. RED-BILLED BLUE MAGPIE
Urocissa erythrorhyncha

192. RUFOUS TREEPIE
Dendrocitta vagabunda

194. HOODED TREEPIE
Crypsirina cucullata

195. HOUSE CROW
Corvus splendens

196. LARGE-BILLED CROW
Corvus macrorhynchos

WOODSWALLOWS Artamini, Corvinae, Corvidae

Two species of woodswallow occur in Myanmar, and both are resident.

Woodswallows are graceful fliers.They differ from true swallows (Hirundinidae) by having broader, more triangular wings and short square tails. They have thick-based, pointed bills. They perch on bare branches or telephone wires. When soaring, they constantly utter a harsh cry. They are gregarious. They feed on insects caught in the air. They nest in trees.

197. ASHY WOODSWALLOW
Artamus fuscus

L 7". A slate-grey bird with bluish bill and whitish upper tail coverts; breast and abdomen, paler. Found in open country and scrub in the plains and foothills, ascending to 5,000 feet. Gregarious. Typically perches on top of tall trees, taking short flights after flying termites and then returning to same perch. Often bobs and fans tail. Social in habits and breeds in colonies. Call: sharp, nasal *mã-ã-ã*, repeated endlessly. Breeds from April to June. Common resident.

ORIOLES, CUCKOOSHRIKES, MINIVETS Oriolini, Corvinae, Covidae

Myanmar has twenty-three species of this group, and nineteen are resident.

Orioles are mostly yellow and black in colour; females are duller. They are birds of the treetops, usually solitary, but sometimes paired. They feed on fruits and insects, and nest in trees.

Cuckooshrikes are mostly grey or black and white, and frequent treetops and subcanopy of forests. They are solitary but sometimes seen in small groups. They feed largely on insects, and nest in trees.

Minivets are mainly bright-coloured; males are chiefly red and females, yellow. They are active and noisy, and small flocks move quickly through treetops. They are insectivorous and nest in trees.

198. SLENDER-BILLED ORIOLE
Oriolus tenuirostris

L 10½". A yellow bird with black nape band; female, much duller with a tinge on back. Found in drier and more open forests of the plains, foothills and higher hills up to 5,000 feet. Solitary or paired. Song is a repeated loud fluty *wip-wi'u' wow' wow* or *wi wi'u wu wu*. Breeds chiefly in May and June. Resident, common in C Myanmar.

199. BLACK-HOODED ORIOLE
Oriolus xanthornus

L 10". A yellow bird with black head and throat and pinkish-red bill; female, duller. Found in forests of the plains and foothills below 3,000 feet. Common in teak forests of Bago Yoma. Song is a fluty *h HWI'UU* and *h wu CHI WU*. Breeds from February to July. Common resident.

200. MAROON ORIOLE
Oriolus traillii

L 10½". Male: maroon plumage with black hood and wings and bluish bill. Female; underparts greyish-white, heavily streaked with black. Found in forests at 2,000–7,000 feet. Shy. A fruit eater, partial to flowering letpan trees. Song is a fluty *pi-loi-lo, pi-oho-uu* etc. Breeds from March to June. Resident, except in Tanintharyi.

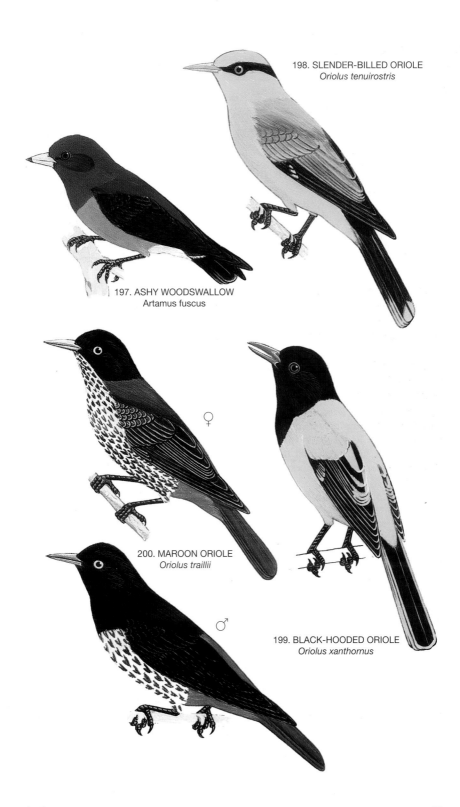

198. SLENDER-BILLED ORIOLE
Oriolus tenuirostris

197. ASHY WOODSWALLOW
Artamus fuscus

♀

200. MAROON ORIOLE
Oriolus traillii

♂

199. BLACK-HOODED ORIOLE
Oriolus xanthornus

201. LARGE CUCKOOSHRIKE
Coracina macei
L 12". A large grey bird with diffuse blackish mask and whitish lower belly and under-tail coverts; female often has faint barring on belly. Found in forest and forest edge up to 7,000 feet. Gregarious. Lifting up each wing alternately and calling simultaneously just after landing on perch, characteristic. Feeds mainly on insects, also on fruits and berries; partial to ficus trees. Call: loud, shrill *kle-eep*. Breeds from April to June. Resident, mostly in mountains.

202. INDOCHINESE CUCKOOSHRIKE
Coracina polioptera
L 9". A dark grey bird with white-tipped tail feathers; female has white eyering and blackish bars on whitish to grey underparts. Found in open forest, secondary growth and gardens at 1000–5,000 feet. Arboreal, usually seen calling on treetops and hunting about among branches. Keeps in pairs or small groups. Call: nasal chuntering *uh' uh' uh' uh'-ik* and *uh' uh' uh' uh'* Breeds from April to July. Endemic resident, except in N Myanmar.

203. ROSY MINIVET
Pericrocotus roseus
L 8". Male: ash grey upper parts with pale chin and rosy belly. Female has grey chin and washed-out yellow belly. Found in forests and secondary growth up to 5,000 feet. Active and noisy, small flocks moving quickly through treetops. May occur in large flocks in winter. Call: whirring trill. Breeds from April onwards. Common resident.

204. SMALL MINIVET
Pericrocotus cinnamomeus
L 6½". A small, long-tailed minivet with flame-coloured patch on rump and wings, also on breast in male. Found in forests of foothills, ascending to 5,000 feet, and fringes of mangroves. Usually in small flocks in treetops. Call: *tswee-eet* and *swee swee*. Breeds from March to June. Common resident, mostly in mountains, except in N Myanmar.

205. GREY-CHINNED MINIVET
Pericrocotus solaris
L 7½". Male: orange-red with grey head and mantle and whitish chin. Female: olive-yellow with grey head and mantle, greyish white chin and yellow patch on dark wings. Found in open forests at 2,000–6,000 feet. Keeps in small parties, often in association with mixed species feeding flocks. Call: *tswee-seet* and *swirrririt*. Breeds from February to April. Resident, except in C Myanmar.

206. SCARLET MINIVET
Pericrocotus flammeus
L 8½". Male, chiefly red and female, yellow. Found in forests of foothills and higher hills up to 6,500 feet. A bird of treetops, gregarious, and regularly joins mixed-species feeding flocks. Often seen in noisy swooping flight with tail fanned. Call: *sweep sweep sweep* and *weep weep weep-wit-wip*. Breeds from April to July. Common resident.

207. BAR-WINGED FLYCATCHER-SHRIKE
Hemipus picatus
L 6". Male: black and dusky white. Female: brown and dusky white. Found in forests of foothills and higher hills up to 7,000 feet. A forest bird. Catches insects on the wing, occasionally seizing them on the ground. Keeps in parties outside breeding season. Call: high-pitched *chir-rup chir-rup*. Breeds from March to July. Common resident.

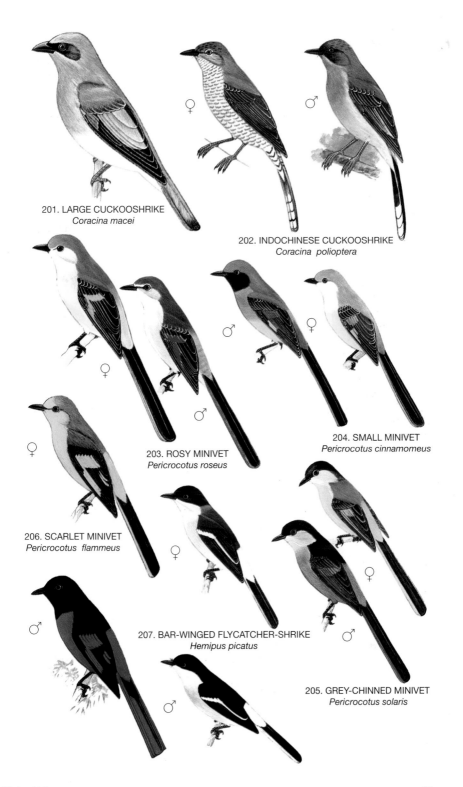

201. LARGE CUCKOOSHRIKE
Coracina macei

202. INDOCHINESE CUCKOOSHRIKE
Coracina polioptera

203. ROSY MINIVET
Pericrocotus roseus

204. SMALL MINIVET
Pericrocotus cinnamomeus

206. SCARLET MINIVET
Pericrocotus flammeus

207. BAR-WINGED FLYCATCHER-SHRIKE
Hemipus picatus

205. GREY-CHINNED MINIVET
Pericrocotus solaris

FANTAILS Rhipidurini, Dicrurinae, Corvidae

Fantails are respresented in Myanmar by four species, and all are resident.

Fantails are slender birds with short, rounded wings and long, broad tails, often distinctly held cocked and fanned. They inhabit undergrowth and trees, associating with mixed species feeding flocks. They are active and inquisitive. They feed mostly on insects caught mid-air. They nest in trees.

208. WHITE-THROATED FANTAIL
Rhipidura albicollis

L 7½". A blackish grey bird with white throat and white eyebrow. Sexes alike. Found in thick scrub in moist forest, bamboo thickets, and hill evergreen forests at 2,000–8000 feet. Individuals seen with hunting parties of small birds. Song is a high-pitched *tsu sit tsu sit sit sit sit tsu*. Breeds in Apirl. Common resident.

209. WHITE-BROWED FANTAIL
Rhipidura aureola

L 7". A brownish grey bird with white eyebrow; forehead, underparts and tail-tip, white. Sexes alike. Found in secondary growth and open deciduous forests up to 3,500 feet. A common and characteristic bird of the Dry Zone of C Myanmar. Strictly arboreal. Song is a melodious *chee chee-cheweechee-vi*. Breeds from April to July. Resident.

DRONGOS Dicrurini, Dicrurinae, Corvidae

Myanmar has eight species of drongo and seven are resident.

Drongos are arboreal birds with glossy black plumage and distinctly shaped tails. They have red eyes. They are bold and pugnacious, and are usually solitary or sometimes seen in pairs. They usually perch in exposed places, such as telephone wires. Most of them move with the season although some are sedentary and territorial. They feed primarily on insects. Sexes are alike.

210. BLACK DRONGO
Dicrurus macrocercus

L 11". A black bird with bluish gloss; tail deeply forked. Found in open country, especially along roadsides, in cultivated areas and in towns up to 4,000 feet. Often seen in association with domestic cattle, snapping up insects disturbed by the animals' movements. Call: *al-cheet* and *al-ka-chi-ri*. Breeds from March to May. Common resident, mostly in lowlands.

211. ASHY DRONGO
Dicrurus leucophaeus

L 11½". A black bird with widely and deeply forked tail. Found in forests of foothills and higher hills, ascending to 8000 feet. A typical bird of teak forest of Bago Yoma in cold weather. Keeps mainly to treetops. Rather shy. Call: *drangh-gip or gip-gip-drangh*. Breeds from March to June. Common resident.

212. BRONZED DRONGO
Dicrurus aeneus

L 9½". A black bird with glossy, metallic blue green sheen. Found in forests of foothills and higher hills, ascending to 6,000 feet. Keeps mainly to treetops. Has a swift and graceful flight. Call: harsh *crer-reate* or *ger-ler-ger-lee*k. Breeds from March to May. Common resident.

208. WHITE-THROATED FANTAIL
Rhipidura albicollis

210. BLACK DRONGO
Dicrurus macrocercus

209. WHITE-BROWED FANTAIL
Rhipidura aureola

211. ASHY DRONGO
Dicrurus leucophaeus

212. BRONZED DRONGO
Dicrurus aeneus

Birds of Myanmar

213. LESSER RACKET-TAILED DRONGO
Dicrurus remifer
L 11" (outer tail feathers 15" extra). A black bird with dense tuft of feathers at base of bill. Found in hill forests, especially along trails and clearings, up to 8,500 feet. Flight slow and dipping, but active when in pursuit of winged termites. Call: loud, musical and very varied, including much mimicry. Breeds from April to June. Common resident.

214. SPANGLED DRONGO
Dicrurus hottentotus
L 13". A black bird with long hair-like feathers springing from forehead and outer tail feathers strongly upturned at tip. Found in forests and secondary growth up to 4,000 feet. Feeds largely by searching flowers, leaves and tree-trunks for insects; also catches insects on the wing. Remarkably fearless when breeding. Call: chit-wiii. Breeds from March to May. Resident and migrant up to 8,000 feet.

215. GREATER RACKET-TAILED DRONGO
Dicrurus paradiseus
L 13". (outer tail feathers 12" extra). A black bird with crest at base of massive bill. Found in open forests of the plains and foothills below 3,000 feet. An arboreal forest bird, common in teak forests of Bago Yoma. Bold, confiding and quite tame. Catches insects by flying out again and again from a fixed tree or from tree to tree. Often seen in small flocks. Call: *tse-rung tse-rung* or a-*hwe-hwe-hwe-hwe-hwe-yo*u. Breeds from March to June. Common resident.

MONARCHS, PARADISE-FLYCATCHERS Monarchini, Dicrurinae, Corvidae
Two species of this group occur in Myanmar, and both are resident.

Monarchs and paradise-flycathers are brightly-coloured birds with longish to very long tails. They have long, ridged bill with a broad flat base. They feed mainly on insects gleaned from foliage.

216. BLACK-NAPED MONARCH
Hypothymis azurea
L 6½". A blue bird with whitish belly; male has black nape and gorget, and female has grey-brown back. Found in bamboo jungle and undergrowth of forests of foothills and higher hills up to 4,000 feet; also occurs in the plains where there is suitable cover. Partial to moist bamboo forest near streams. Usually solitary. Song is a clear, monotonous, ringing *wii wii wii wii wii wii*. Breeds from April to June. Common resident.

217. ASIAN PARADISE -FLYCATCHER
Terpsiphone paradisi
L 8¾". Male: either white or rufous with black head and 9" elongate tail. Female: rufous with black crown. Found in dry forests of C Myanmar; also in gardens, mangroves and evergreen hill forests up to 4,000 feet. Active and conspicuous. Upright posture when perched. Feeds entirely on insects caught on the wing. Song is a clear rolling *chu' wu wu wu wu wu*. Breeds from March to August. Resident.

IROAS Acgithininae, Corvidae
Myanmar has three species of iora, and all are resident.

Ioras are small, robust birds with mostly green and yellow fluffy plumage. They have stout bills and fairly short tails. They are active and restless, hopping and jumping in foliage with acrobatic postures as they hunt for insects. They are usually paired. They nest in trees.

213. LESSER RACKET-TAILED DRONGO
Dicrurus remifer

214. SPANGLED DRONGO
Dicrurus hottentotus

215. GREATER RACKET-TAILED DRONGO
Dicrurus paradiseus

216. BLACK-NAPED MONARCH
Hypothymis azurea

217. ASIAN PARADISE -FLYCATCHER
Terpsiphone paradisi

218. COMMON IORA
Aegithina tiphia
L 6". A green and yellow bird with two white wing-bars. Found in gardens and compounds, also in outskirts of villages and cultivations, forest edge and scrub jungle below 3,000 feet. Most common in Dry Zone of C Myanmar. Usually solitary. Song is a thin drawn-out *whiiiiii piu*. Breeds from April to September. Common resident, except in hills of N Myanmar.

WOODSHRIKES Vangini, Maiaconotinae, Corvidae
The Woodshrikes are represented in Myanmar by four species, and all are resident.

Woodshrikes are brownish and whitish in colour, with stout bills. They are rather sluggish and slow-moving, and inhabit relatively open areas. They usually move about in small parties in treetops. They feed mainly on insects. Sexes are alike.

219. LARGE WOODSHRIKE
Tephrodornis gularis
L 9". A brownish grey bird with blackish mask. Found in forests of foothills and higher hills up to 6,000 feet. Common in teak forests of Bago Yoma during cold season. A very noisy bird. Usually seen in small parties in treetops, moving from tree to tree with a slow dipping flight. Call: musical *kee-a kee-a*, harsh chreek chreek chreek. Breeds from March to May. Common resident.

220. COMMON WOODSHRIKE
Tephrodornis pondicerianus
L 6½". A brownish grey bird with blackish mask. Found in open wooded country and scrub jungle up to 5,000 feet. Commonest in C and E Myanmar. Seen in small parties in treetops. Call: whistled *wheet wheet,whi whi whi whi*. Breeds from February to July. Resident.

THRUSHES, SHORTWINGS Turdinae, Muscicapidae
Myanmar has twenty-five species of this group and twelve are resident.

Thrushes and shortwings differ widely in habits and appearances.

Typical thrushes (*Zoothera, Turdus*) are relatively large in size with strong legs and bills, and they are adapted to living on the ground; they feed on insects, worms, berries and fallen fruits. Rock thrushes (*Monticola*) are noted for upright posture; they favour tall rocks, trees and buildings of open areas, and fly with rapid wing beats in a jerky fashion. Whistling thrushes (Myophonus) live on the ground along forest streams, feeding on aquatic insects, beetles, snails and berries. Shortwings (*Brachypteryx*) are small birds with short rounded wings and relatively short tails; they feed mainly on insects.

221. CHESTNUT-BELLIED ROCK THRUSH
Monticola rufiventris
L 9½". Male: upper parts blue, sides of head, chin, neck and throat, black and rest of underparts, chestnut. Female: barred brownish plumage with plain buff throat. Found in open forests at 3,000–8,000 feet. Usually seen perched high up on tree, jerking tail backwards and forward over back. Song is a quite rich undulating series of short warbling, whistled phrases. Breeds from May to June. Resident in W, N and E Myanmar.

218. COMMON IORA
Aegithina tiphia

220. COMMON WOODSHRIKE
Tephrodornis pondicerianus

219. LARGE WOODSHRIKE
Tephrodornis gularis

221. CHESTNUT-BELLIED ROCK THRUSH
Monticola rufiventris

222. BLUE WHISTLING THRUSH
Myophonus caeruleus

L 13". A dark purplish-blue bird with yellow to black bill. Sexes alike. Found along forest streams of foothills and higher hills up to 10,000 feet. Bold and conspicuous. Feeds on berries, water beetles and vegetable matter. Song is a pleasant mixture of mellow fluty and harsh scratchy notes. Breeds from February to August. Common resident.

223. LESSER SHORTWING
Brachypteryx leucophrys

L 5". An olive-brown bird with whitish throat and centre of abdomen. Sexes alike. Found in dense evergreen forests at 3,000–8,000 feet. Shy and secretive. Keeps in pairs, creeping about stumps and the tangle of fallen trees on forest floor. Song is brief, high-pitched and melodious. Breeds from March to June. Resident in W, N and E Myanmar and Tanintharyi.

FLYCATCHERS Muscicapidae

Thirty-one species of flycatcher occur in Myanmar and twenty-four are resident.

Flycatchers are mainly insect-eating birds, living among trees. They have weak legs, and their beaks are short and flat with long bristles at the gape. They are solitary or paired. They usually fly out from a high perch, catch the prey in the air and then return to their starting point. Some species are skulkers and glean insects from inside the foliage. Sexes often differ, with brightly coloured males and duller brownish females. Some are migratory, but most are sedentary residents. They nest in trees.

224. SNOWY-BROWED FLYCATCHER
Ficedula hyperythra

L 4½". Male: slaty-blue above and orange-rufous below, with white eyebrow. Female: brown with short eyebrow. Found in evergreen hill forests above 3,000 feet along small streams. Seen both in trees and on ground. Usually tame and confiding, but shy during nesting. Song is almost a wheeze, *tsit-sit-si-sii,tsi-sii-swrri* and *tsi-sii'i*. Breeds from April to June. Resident.

225. LITTLE PIED FLYCATCHER
Ficedula westermanni

L 4½". Male: black above, white below with white eyebrow. Female: greyish above, white below. Found in forests and forest edge above 3,000 feet. Not shy. Keeps to undergrowth. Lively and always on the move. Song is thin, sweet and high-pitched, often followed by a rattled call note. Breeds from March to July. Resident.

226. VERDITER FLYCATCHER
Eumyias thalassina

L 6½". A greenish blue bird; female, duller; lores, black in male, dusky in female. Found in open forests and gardens up to 7,000 feet; also in foothills and wooded plains in winter. Usually in small groups. Not shy and perches conspicuously. Hawks insects in air, also catches them in foliage. Song loud and pleasant in breeding season, quiet at other times. Breeds from April to July. Resident, except in C and S Myanmar.

222. BLUE WHISTLING THRUSH
Myophonus caeruleus

223. LESSER SHORTWING
Brachypteryx leucophrys

224. SNOWY-BROWED FLYCATCHER
Ficedula hyperythra

225. LITTLE PIED FLYCATCHER
Ficedula westermanni

226. VERDITER FLYCATCHER
Eumyias thalassina

227. LARGE NILTAVA
Niltava grandis

L 8½". Male: deep blue with brilliant blue crown, rump, upper tail coverts and wing patch. Female: brown, paler below. Found in dense evergreen forests of higher hills above 3,000 feet. Favours lower trees in densest parts of forest. Quite confiding. Feeds mainly on insects caught on ground. Song is a softly whistled *uu-uu-du-di*. Breeds from April to July. Resident, except in SW, C and S Myanmar.

228. TICKELL'S BLUE FLYCATCHER
Cyornis tickelliae

L 6". A blue bird with orange-rufous breast and white belly; female, paler and duller. Found in wooded areas, bamboo jungles and gardens below 2,000 feet. Song consists of quite slowly delivered sweet, high-pitched slightly descending phrases. Breeds from April to August. Resident, except in C and S Myanmar.

229. GREY-HEADED CANARY FLYCATCHER
Culicicapa ceylonensis

L 5". A bright olive-green bird with grey head and yellow belly. Found in forests of higher hills up to 8,000 feet; common in foothills during cold weather. A typical bird of teak forest of Bago Yoma in cold season. Solitary, but often seen in bird waves. Frequently fans tail. Feeds on insects caught in flight. Song is a loud clear trill followed by a prolonged twittering note. Breeds in March and April. Common resident.

CHATS and allies Saxicolini, Muscicapinae, Muscicapidae

Myanmar has thirty-six species of this group and twenty-three are resident.

Chats favour low bushes or grass stems of open country. They usually adopt upright posture. They continually flick tail up, simultaneously fanning it open, and jerking wings. They nest in holes or crevices of walls or banks, sometimes directly on ground.

Robins and redstarts inhabit the undergrowth, forest floor and rocky stream beds. They are shy and secretive , and characteristically cock tail, frequently opening and closing it. They feed on insects usually caught on ground or in low bushes. They nest in tree holes, steep banks or rocks.

Forktails are black and white in colour with deeply forked tails. They live along rocky streams and feed on insects caught in the water. They nest among the rocks.

230. ORIENTAL MAGPIE ROBIN
Copsychus saularis

L 8½". A black and white bird with the tail often lowered and expanded, then closed and jerked up again over the back. Found in the plains, foothills and higher hills up to 5,500 feet, frequenting gardens, cultivated areas, brush, mangroves and cities. One of the most familiar birds all over the country. Solitary or paired. Feeds on the ground. Song is loud, melodious and varied. Breeds from March to July. Common resident.

231. WHITE-RUMPED SHAMA
Copsychus malabaricus

L 11". A blackish bird with orange rufous underparts. Found in forests of foothills, ascending locally to 5,000 feet. A typical bird of teak forests. Shy and keeps to undergrowth. Cocks tail, especially when landing on perch. Feeds mostly on the ground. Song is loud and beautiful with a varied range of notes. Breeds from March to May. Common resident, mostly in lowlands.

227. LARGE NILTAVA
Niltava grandis

228. TICKELL'S BLUE FLYCATCHER
Cyornis tickelliae

229. GREY-HEADED CANARY FLYCATCHER
Culicicapa ceylonensis

230. ORIENTAL MAGPIE ROBIN
Copsychus saularis

231. WHITE-RUMPED SHAMA
Copsychus malabaricus

232. BLACK-BACKED FORKTAIL
Enicurus immaculatus
L 9". A black and white bird with narrow white band on fore-crown; back, plain black. Sexes alike. Found on forest streams of foothills up to 2,500 feet. A typical bird of teak forests along rocky streams. Call: whistled *wheat wheat*. Breeds from end of March to May. Resident, except in Tanintharyi.

233. SLATY-BACKED FORKTAIL
Enicurus schistaceus
L 10". A black and white bird with long forked tail and greyish blue crown and back. Sexes alike. Found on larger rocky streams in scrub and forested country of foothills and higher hills up to 7,000 feet. Usually in pairs or small groups. Call: sharp, high-pitched metallic *chick*. Breeds from February to June. Resident, except in SW Myanmar.

234. WHITE-CROWNED FORKTAIL
Enicurus leschenaulti
L 11". A large black and white bird with long forked tail, white forehead and crown and black breast. Sexes alike. Found on smaller rocky streams of dense evergreen forsests of mountains and foothills. Usually in pairs or small groups. Song is a high-pitched tsswi'i'i'lli'i'i' etc. Breeds from April to October. Resident, except in C Myanmar.

235. COMMON STONECHAT
Saxicola torquata
L 5½". Male: head, wings and tail, black and breast, orange-rufous. Female: dull brown. Found in open country, in paddy plains and grasslands. Usually in pairs. Hawks insects by short sorties from perch or traps them on the ground. Continuously spreads and wags tail when perched. Flight low and jerky. Song is a variable, rather scratchy series of twittering, warbling notes. Breeds from March to July. Resident in N Myanmar and winter visitor throughout the plains, from mid-August to mid-May.

236. PIED BUSHCHAT
Saxicola caprata
L 5½". Male: black with white rump. Female: dark brown with rusty rump. Found in open country in secondary growth, hedges and cultivations, but not in paddy plains. Takes most of its food from the ground, flying down to it and then returning to perch. Also catches flying insects on the wing. Song is a short, but pleasing *hiu hiu hiu-u'wee'wipee'chiu* etc. Breeds from March to August. Goes up to the hills (5,000 feet) to breed. Resident.

237. GREY BUSHCHAT
Saxicola ferrea
L 6". Male: blue-grey upper parts with black cheek, wide white eyebrow and white wing bar in breeding plumage, browner in non-breeding plumage. Female: dark brown with indistinct whitish eyebrow, without wing patch. Found in open country, open forests of higher hills and neighbourhood of man up to 7,000 feet. Mainly a mountain bird. Often perches on top of bush or in trees. Song is a pretty *titheratu-chak-lew-titatit*. Breeds from March to June. Resident, except in C Myanmar and Tanintharyi.

232. BLACK-BACKED FORKTAIL
Enicurus immaculatus

235. COMMON STONECHAT
Saxicola torquata

233. SLATY-BACKED FORKTAIL
Enicurus schistaceus

234. WHITE-CROWNED FORKTAIL
Enicurus leschenaulti

237. GREY BUSHCHAT
Saxicola ferrea

236. PIED BUSHCHAT
Saxicola caprata

STARLINGS, MYNAS Sturnidae

Seventeen species of this family occur in Myanmar and eleven are resident.

Starlings and mynas are stocky, medium-sized birds with strong, pointed bills, strong legs and relatively short tails. Their flight is strong and direct, many showing white wing patches. Many species frequently walk on the ground. They are gregarious, aggressive and bold and very noisy. Their calls are loud and raucous, but some species have pleasing whistles. They feed on insects and fruits, and nest in colonies.

238. CHESTNUT-TAILED STARLING
Sturnus malabaricus

L 8". A small pale grey starling with blue-based, yellow-tipped bill and chestnut-rufous outer tail feathers. Found in open forests, gardens and paddy fields throughout the plains and foothills, ascending to 4,000 feet. Arboreal and active. Usually in flocks. Breeds from April to June. Resident.

239. ASIAN PIED STARLING
Sturnus contra

L 9½". A conspicuously pied starling with orange bill and bare orbital skin. Found in the plains in paddy fields and cultivations. Not found in higher hills and forests, but more rural than Common Myna. Roosts and nests in kokko trees along bunded roads. Breeds from May to August. Common resident.

240. BLACK-COLLARED STARLING
Sturnus nigricollis

L 11". A dark brown starling with black neck collar. Found in open country in cultivations, scrub and paddy fields up to 5,000 feet. Spends most of its time on ground, picking up grasshoppers and crickets. Usually in pairs, but in large groups at roosting time. Breeds from April to June. Common resident.

241. VINOUS-BREASTED STARLING
Sturnus burmannicus

L 10". A dark grey starling with white head and wine-coloured breast and belly. Found in open grasslands, gardens, cultivations and scrub jungle of Dry Zone of C Myanmar. Roosts in reeds, sugar-cane, bamboo clumps or similar cover. Nests in tree holes, under eaves of houses or in roofs of thatched huts. Breeds from April to June. Endemic resident.

242. COMMON MYNA
Acridotheres tristis

L 10". A dark brown myna with blackish grey head, neck and upper breast and bright yellow facial skin. Found in open country, cultivations, towns and villages up to 5,000 feet. Rarely seen far from towns and villages. Usually paired. Terrestrial, picking up insects, seeds and fruits, also kitchen scraps. Breeds from April to October. Common resident.

243. JUNGLE MYNA
Acridotheres fuscus

L 9½". A dark greyish brown myna with short crest and yellow-tipped blue bill. Found in the plains in open country, in cities, paddy fields, gardens, forest clearings and mangroves. Often seen in association with cattle and buffaloes. Breeds from February to July. Resident, except in N Myanmar.

239. ASIAN PIED STARLING
Sturnus contra

238. CHESTNUT-TAILED STARLING
Sturnus malabaricus

240. BLACK-COLLARED STARLING
Sturnus nigricollis

241. VINOUS-BREASTED STARLING
Sturnus burmannicus

242. COMMON MYNA
Acridotheres tristis

243. JUNGLE MYNA
Acridotheres fuscus

244. WHITE-VENTED MYNA
Acridotheres grandis
L 10". A black myna with crest on forehead, yellow bill, reddish eyes and white under tail coverts. Found in open country in paddy fields and cities up to 5,000 feet. A familiar bird around Yangon in breeding season. Often perches on cattle. Breeds from April to August. Resident, except in SW Myanmar.

245. HILL MYNA
Gracula religiosa
L 12". A popular cage bird. Found in forests of the foothills, ascending to 4,500 feet. Sociable, usually seen in large parties in treetops. A characteristic bird of teak forests of Bago Yoma. Primarily arboreal, seldom seen on the ground. Breeds from April to June. Resident.

NUTHATCHES Sittidae
This family is represented in Myanmar by seven species.

Nuthatches are non-migratory birds. They are small with short tails and sharply pointed bills. Like woodpeckers, they climb about tree trunks and branches but in jerky hops and search for insects and spiders; most also take a certain amount of nuts and fruits. They nest in tree hollows, often plastering entrance with mud to reduce the opening. The nest site is often close to the ground.

246. CHESTNUT-BELLIED NUTHATCH
Sitta castanea
L 5½". A blue-grey bird with chestnut underparts. Found in forests, secondary growth and gardens up to 5,000 feet. Sociable, often seen in mixed parties. Sometimes feeds on ground on ants and termites. Call: *cheep-cheep-cheep* etc. Breeds from March to April. Resident, usually in lowlands.

247. WHITE-BROWED NUTHATCH
Sitta victoriae
L 5". An endemic resident found on Natmataung (Mt. Victoria) in Chin Hills at 7,500–9,200 feet. Female is much duller and paler than the male. Call: *pit* or *plit* and *pee pee pee pee*. Breeds in April. Fairly common (U Shein Gay Ngai, Park Warden, 2000, *pers. comm.*)

248. VELVET-FRONTED NUTHATCH
Sitta frontalis
L 5". A violet-blue nuthatch with coral-red bill and velvety black patch on forehead. Found in all types of forests in the plains, foothills and higher hills up to 6,000 feet. Often hunts in small parties constantly calling to each other with a mouse-like squeaking. Call: *chwit-chwit*. Breeds from February to April. Resident.

TREECREEPERS Certhiidae
Myanmar has four species of treecreepers, and all are resident.

Treecreepers are small, streaky brown birds with downcurved bills and greatly graduated tails. They creep up tree trunks and along branches, often starting at the bottom of tree. They are solitary or paired, often seen with a mixed hunting party of tits and warblers. They feed on insects and larvae picked up from crevices of the bark. They nest in holes of tree trunks.

244. WHITE-VENTED MYNA
Acridotheres grandis

245. HILL MYNA
Gracula religiosa

246. CHESTNUT-BELLIED NUTHATCH
Sitta castanea

247. WHITE-BROWED NUTHATCH
Sitta victoriae

248. VELVET-FRONTED NUTHATCH
Sitta frontalis

249. BROWN-THROATED TREECREEPER
Certhia discolor

L 6½". A streaky brown bird with grey-brown throat, breast and belly and rofous brown tail; under tail coverts, rufous buff. Found in mountain forests, usually above 4,500 feet. Sometimes, associates with mixed-species feeding flocks. Song is a rather loud chee-weet chee-weet chee-weet chee-weet. Breeds from January to July. Resident in W, N, S and E Myanmar.

TITS Paridae, Aegithalidae

Twelve species of Tit occur in Myanmar and eleven are resident.

Tits are small, plump, thick-necked, stumpy-billed birds, living in all types of wooded areas. They are active and sprightly in their movements, usually moving about in noisy flocks, sometimes accompanying mixed flocks of babblers and warblers. They gently flick the wings and tails as they move about, often in acrobatic posture clinging upside down to leaves and twigs. They feed mainly on trees, and sometimes on ground, foraging amongst fallen leaves and debris for insects, larvae, seeds and berries. Most species build nests in tree holes.

250. GREAT TIT
Parus major

L 5". A greyish green bird with black head, throat and upper breast, and a black line running down centre of white underparts. Found in forests of the plains, foothills and higher hills (rare in higher hills). Arboreal and acrobatic. Call: *tsee-tsee-tsee*. Breeds from February to May. Resident, except in Tanintharyi.

251. YELLOW-CHEEKED TIT
Parus spilonotus

L 5½". A greyish bird with black crest and yellow cheeks. Found in forests of higher hills at 3,000–7,000 feet. Usually paired. Associates with mixed species hunting parties in undergrowth and lower canopy. Call: *sit-si-si-si, tsee-tsee-tsee* etc. Breeds from March to June. Resident, except in C Myanmar.

252. SULTAN TIT
Melanochlora sultanea

L 8". A black and yellow bird with yellow crest. Found in forests and secondary growth in the plains and foothills below 3,000 feet. Usually in pairs or small parties. Slower in movement than other tits. Keeps to treetops in moist and evergreen forests, occasionally visiting more open country. Call: shrill *chip-tree-tree* etc. Breeds from Apirl to July. Resident.

253. BLACK-THROATED TIT
Aegithalos concinnus

L 4". A greyish bird with chestnut crown, black throat patch and longish tail. Found in forests of higher hills above 3,000 feet. Usually in small parties. Equally at home in branches of high trees in thick forest and amongst bushes of open, grassy hillsides. Call: thin *psip pisp* and *sibilant si si si si* etc. Breeds from March to May.Resident in W N and E Myanmar.

249. BROWN-THROATED TREECREEPER
Certhia discolor

250. GREAT TIT
Parus major

♀

♂

251. YELLOW-CHEEKED TIT
Parus spilonotus

♀

252. SULTAN TIT
Melanochlora sultanea

♂

253. BLACK-THROATED TIT
Aegithalos concinnus

Birds of Myanmar

99

MARTINS, SWALLOWS Hirundinidae

This family is represented in Myanmar by eleven species and six are resident.

Martins and swallows are distinguished from swifts by their shorter, broader wings and more fluttering flight. They are wonderful fliers and feed on insects which they take in the air over open land and lakes. They are gregarious, and often perch in the open on telephone wires or trees. They roost communally in large numbers outside breeding season. They nest in natural hollows or excavate their own burrows or build mud-nests which they plaster on to cliff ridges, buildings etc. Most live in neighbourhood of man. Sexes are alike.

254. PLAIN MARTIN
Riparia paludicola

L 4½". A brownish bird with whitish lower breast and belly. Found in marshes and on rivers, especially near sandbanks. Gregarious at all times. Feeds chiefly over water. Roosts in reed beds. Nests in river banks and banks of lakes and ponds. Call: *chrr'r, chit chit chit* or *chut chut chut*. Breeds from November to June in colonies. Not found in south Tanintharyi. Resident below 3,000 feet.

255. BARN SWALLOW
Hirundo rustica

L 6" (outer tail feathers 2" to 5" more). A steel blue bird with white to chestnut underparts and chestnut throat and forehead; tail deeply forked. Found in cities, villages and open areas, often near water. Migrant up to 8,000 feet. Large flocks roost on bare sandbanks of larger rivers where they may be seen at dawn and dusk. Since adults arrive in July and juveniles leave in June, they are seen in every month of the year. Call: *vit*, often repeated. Winter visitor.

256. WIRE-TAILED SWALLOW
Hirundo smithii

L 5" (outer tail feathers up to 5" more). A glossy blue-black bird with chestnut crown and pure white underparts. Found on rivers and lakes and in wet paddy fields below 6,000 feet. Keeps in pairs or small parties (not in large flocks). Flight exceptionally fast and powerful. Perches freely on telephone wires and parapets of bridges, but not on trees. Call: *chit-chit, chirrik-weet chirrik-weet*. Breeds from March to May, sometimes till September. Resident.

257. STRIATED SWALLOW
Hirundo striolata

L 7" (outer tail feathers up to 1" more). A glossy blue-black bird with chestnut rump and whitish streaked underparts. Found in open areas. Favours sandy river beds, cultivations and scrubjungle in the plains. Often associates with house martins in the hills, or with house swallows. Call: *cheenk, quitsch, pin* etc. Breeds from February to September. Resident in N, C, S and E Myanmar and Tanintharyi.

BULBULS Pycnonotidae

Myanmar has thirty-three species of bulbul, and all are resident.

Bulbuls are arboreal birds with soft plumage. They are gregarious, and bold and confiding. They are vocal, and most have pleasant songs and often harsh calls. They feed on fruits. Sometimes several species feed together on fruiting trees. Some are familiar birds of towns and gardens, whereas others are only seen in forests; forest species usually keep to middle storey. Sexes are alike.

256. WIRE-TAILED SWALLOW
Hirundo smithii

255. BARN SWALLOW
Hirundo rustica

254. PLAIN MARTIN
Riparia paludicola

257. STRIATED SWALLOW
Hirundo striolata

258. BLACK-HEADED BULBUL
Pycnonotus atriceps

L 7". An olive and yellow bird with crestless black head; tail, yellow-tipped with dark brown subterminal band. Found in forests, secondary growth, stream sides and coastal scrub. Frequents both dense and open forests. Equally at home in treetops and undergrowth. Feeds on fruits, berries and small insects. Song is a series of short, spaced, tuneless whistles. Breeds in April and May. Resident up to 8,000 feet, mostly below 3,000 feet, except in N Myanmar.

259. BLACK-CRESTED BULBUL
Pycnonotus melanicterus

L 7½". An olive and yellow bird with black head and crest. Found in forest edge, secondary growth and scrub up to 5,000 feet. A characteristic bird of teak forests, seen chiefly in small clearings and along streams. Song is a cheerful quick *whitu-whirru-wheet, whit-whaet-ti-whaet* and *whi-wiu*. Breeds from March to May. Common resident.

260. RED-WHISKERED BULBUL
Pycnonotus jocosus

L 8". A brownish bird with white underparts and tall, erect crest. Found in the plains and foothills in gardens, cultivations, scrub jungle and neighbourhood of villages up to 5,000 feet. Avoids high forests. Most gregarious of all bulbuls. Song consists of musical *wit-ti-waet, queep kwil-ya, queek-kay*. Breeds from February to June. Common resident.

261. RED-VENTED BULBUL
Pycnonotus cafer

L 9". A blackish bird with red vent and full crest. Found in the plains and foothills in gardens, cultivations, scrub jungle and secondary growth up to 5,000 feet. Avoids high forests. Often collects in large flocks to feed on flowering trees. Song is a cheerful be careful or be quick quick. Breeds from February to May. Resident, except in Tanintharyi.

262. FLAVESCENT BULBUL
Pycnonotus flavescens

L 8½". A greyish-brown bird with yellow under tail coverts. Found in scrub jungles of higher hills and open high forests at 3,000–8,500 feet. The commonest species of the hill bulbuls in Myanmar. Song is a jolly *joi whiti-whiti-wit* etc. Breeds from March to June, mainly in April. Common resident, except in C Myanmar.

263. STREAK-EARED BULBUL
Pycnonotus blanfordi

L 8". An ashy-grey bird, rather nondescript, of the plains. Found in gardens, cultivations, coastal scrub and secondary growth up to 3,000 feet. Avoids forests. Call: harsh, rasping which which which and piping brink brink brink. Breeds from March to August. Common endemic resident, except in Tanintharyi and N Myanmar, commoner in C Myanmar.

264. OLIVE BULBUL
Iole virescens

L 7½". An olive-green bird with white-streaked head and dark reddish to brown eyes; yellower below and stronger olive above. Found in forests of the foothills in most parts of the country. Keeps in noisy parties hunting through bamboo thickets or tree canopy. Call: musical *whe-ic*. Breeds from March to June. Resident up to 3,000 feet.

258. BLACK-HEADED BULBUL
Pycnonotus atriceps

259. BLACK-CRESTED BULBUL
Pycnonotus melanicterus

260. RED-WHISKERED BULBUL
Pycnonotus jocosus

261. RED-VENTED BULBUL
Pycnonotus cafer

263. STREAK-EARED BULBUL
Pycnonotus blanfordi

262. FLAVESCENT BULBUL
Pycnonotus flavescens

264. OLIVE BULBUL
Iole virescens

Birds of Myanmar

265. ASHY BULBUL
Hemixos flavala
L 8". A dark, ashy bird with black crown, brown ear coverts, whitish throat and under-parts and bright yellow wing-patch. Found in forests and secondary growth at 2,000–6,000 feet (sometimes lower). Keeps in noisy parties working their way through lower canopy or top of undergrowth and bamboo thickets. Song is a simple, repeated, rather high-pitched *ii-wit'ti-ui* etc. Breeds from May to July. Resident.

266. MOUNTAIN BULBUL
Hypsipetes mcclellandii
L 9½". An olive-green bird with brown erectile crest and white-streaked crown and throat; belly, white to buff. Found in evergreen and wet oak forests in higher hills at 3,000–8,500 feet. Purely a forest bird and does not enter open country. Call: shrill, squawking *cheu* or *tschew* and *tchi-chitu*. Breeds from March to June. Common resident.

267. BLACK BULBUL
Hypsipetes leucocephalus
L 10". A polymorphic species. Subspecies concolor has black plumage with red bill and feet. Subspecies stresemanni has white head. Subspecies leucothorax has both head and breast white. Found in forests of higher hills. Keeps in pairs, small parties or frequently in large parties, foraging in treetops, rarely descending to undergrowth. Song is a discordant but measured series of trip *wi tit-i-whi* etc. Breeds from April to June. Resident / migrant.

CISTICOLAS, PRINIAS and allies Cisticolidae
This family is represented in Myanmar by nine species and all are resident.

Cisticolas, prinias and allies are small, warbler-like birds. They live in marshy and open areas, and feed mainly on insects.

268. ZITTING CISTICOLA
Cisticola juncidis
L 4½". A minute bird with black and brown streaks; underparts, whitish; tail, short and fan-shaped. Found in paddy fields, grass, brush etc in the plains. Skulker, hides until flushed. During breeding season, male performs distinctive undulating display flight, usually over nest. Song is a long monotonous, *clicking dzip dzip dzip dzip* or *pip pip pip pip*. Breeds from May to September. Common resident.

269. RUFESCENT PRINIA
Prinia rufescens
L 4¾". A rufescent brown bird with narrow supercillium; underparts, creamy white. Found in grass, thickets and scrub up to 5,500 feet; less common in higher hills. Keeps in small, lively parties. Flight weak. Creeps among thickets in search of insects. Some-times seen on ground. Song is a rhythmic *ti-chew ti-chew ti-chew ti-chew* or *chewp chewp chewp chewp chewp*. Breeds from January to September. Common resident.

270. GREY-BREASTED PRINIA
Prinia hodgsonii
L 4¾". A tiny grey bird with whitish underparts. Found in grassy undergrowth and scrub jungle; occasionally in paddy fields and swamps. Keeps in parties, creeping in and out of bushes, running like mice on ground. Song is a musical *chiwee chiwee chiwee chip chip chip chip*. Breeds from June to August in the plains; from April to June in the hills up to 5,000 feet. Common resident.

265. ASHY BULBUL
Hemixos flavala

266. MOUNTAIN BULBUL
Hypsipetes mcclellandii

267. BLACK BULBUL
Hypsipetes leucocephalus

268. ZITTING CISTICOLA
Cisticola juncidis

269. RUFESCENT PRINIA
Prinia rufescens

270. GREY-BREASTED PRINIA
Prinia hodgsonii

271. YELLOW-BELLIED PRINIA
Prinia flaviventris
L 51". A dark greenish bird with whitish throat and breast and yellow belly and under tail coverts. Found in reedbeds, swamps and scrub up to 4,000 feet. An active bird, hopping and climbing about the grass in pursuit of insects. Flight weak. Song is a rhythmic *didli-idli-u didli-idli-u didli-idli-u*. Breeds from June to September. Common resident.

272. PLAIN PRINIA
Prinia inornata
L 6". A dark brown bird with whitish creamy supercillium; underparts, pale rufescent buff. Found in the plains in reeds, grass, thickets and paddy fields; often away from water in foothills and grazing grounds; also occurs near houses and in gardens. Goes up to 3,000 feet in Shan State. Song is a monotonous *jit-it jit-it jit-it jit-it jit-it jit-it* or *jirt jirt jirt jirt jirt jirt*. Breeds from March to September. Common resident.

WHITE-EYES Zosteropidae
Three species of this family occur in Myanmar, and one is resident.

White-eyes are small arboreal birds, mainly olive-green and yellow in colour and are easily recognized by a white ring around the eye. They live in flocks in bushes and trees. They feed on nectar, small fruits and insects. They build cup nests in the forks of horizontal branches.

273. ORIENTAL WHITE-EYE
Zosterops palpebrosus
L 4½". An olive-green bird with yellow median stripe on lower breast and belly. Found in forests, secondary growth, scrub, cultivation, and gardens up to 5,000 feet; also in mangroves. Seldom remains long in any particular tree and never descends to the ground. Often mixes with other species. Call: *jeww jeww jeww* or *cheuw cheuw cheuw*. Breeds from March to July. Common resident.

TESIAS, WARBLERS, TAILORBIRDS and allies Acrocephalinae, Sylviidae
Myanmar has sixty species of this group, and thirty-two are resident.

Warblers are small birds with elongated bodies and thin beaks. Most of them are brown without distinguishing features. They live in trees, bushes or reeds and hunt among leaves and twigs for insects which are almost their sole food. They sing beautifully. Sexes are usually similar.

274. SLATY-BELLIED TESIA
Tesia olivea
L 3½". A small olive-green bird with golden olive crown, slate-grey underparts and tailless appearance. Found in evergreen forests. Often seen along watercourses. Keeps to the ground and low undergrowth. Will not fly except under great pressure. Song surprisingly loud. Resident, except in C Myanmar.

275. GREY-BELLIED TESIA
Tesia cyaniventer
L 3½". A small, dark olive-green bird with yellowish supercillium; underparts grey. Found in evergreen forests. Keeps close to the ground. Skulks in undergrowth. Frequents higher elevations in breeding season. Resident, except in C Myanmar.

273. ORIENTAL WHITE-EYE
Zosterops palpebrosus

271. YELLOW-BELLIED PRINIA
Prinia flaviventris

272. PLAIN PRINIA
Prinia inornata

274. SLATY-BELLIED TESIA
Tesia olivea

275. GREY-BELLIED TESIA
Tesia cyaniventer

276. THICK-BILLED WARBLER
Acrocephalus aedon

L 7½". An olive-brown bird, paler below. Found in grass reeds and scrub near marshes, canals and paddy fields. Skulks in bushes and scrub jungle, and partial to bizat along streams. When alarmed, hides inside dense thickets. Winter visitor.

277. MOUNTAIN TAILORBIRD
Orthotomus cuculatus

L 4½". A small greenish bird with orange rufous crown and white eyebrow; throat, white and belly and vent, yellow. Found in dense bamboo thickets and scrub at 3,500–9,000 feet. Keeps in small parties. Shy. Breeds from February to April. Resident, except in SW and C Myanmar.

278. COMMON TAILORBIRD
Orthotomus sutorius

L 4¾". An olive-green bird with rufous forecrown; male has elongated tail feathers. Found in the plains and foothills in gardens and undergrowth, often ascending to 4,000 feet. Frequents undergrowth in forests and scrub jungle. Not shy, and very active. A common bird of gardens in Yangon. Breeds from April to October. Common resident.

279. DARK-NECKED TAILORBIRD
Orthotomus atrogularis

L 5". An olive-green bird with rufous crown and nape and yellow under tail coverts; male has black throat. Found in forest undergrowth, scrub and bamboo thickets up to 5,000 feet. A shy timorous bird. Avoids gardens and open country. Breeds from February to September. Common resident, except in W and C Myanmar.

280. DUSKY WARBLER
Phylloscopus fuscatus

L 5". A dark brown bird with rusty buff eyebrow; underparts, whitish. Found in bush and scurb-jungle near paddy fields, marshes and swampy areas and in mangroves. A skulker, feeding on or near the ground.Winter visitor.

281. YELLOW-BROWED WARBLER
Phylloscopus inornatus

L 4½". An olive-green bird with broad yellowish-white supercillium and white double wing bars. Found in forests and wooded areas, including gardens from the plains to 8,000 feet. Keeps to treetops. Winter visitor, mid-October to mid-April.

282. GREENISH WARBLER
Phylloscopus trochiloides

L 4¾". A dark olive bird with one narrow wing bar; underparts, sullied white. Found in open forests, especially bamboo up to 5,000 feet, but chiefly of the plains. Arboreal. Winter visitor. Likely to be resident in N Myanmar.

283. TWO-BARRED WARBLER
Phylloscopus plumbeitarsus

L 4¾". A dark olive bird with two yellowish-white wing bars. Found in mixed deciduous and semi-evergreen forests and bamboo jungle; parks and gardens during migration. Active, foraging in mid-storey foliage. Winter visitor.

276. THICK-BILLED WARBLER
Acrocephalus aedon

277. MOUNTAIN TAILORBIRD
Orthotomus cuculatus

♀

♂

278. COMMON TAILORBIRD
Orthotomus sutorius

♀

♂

279. DARK-NECKED TAILORBIRD
Orthotomus atrogularis

281. YELLOW-BROWED WARBLER
Phylloscopus inornatus

280. DUSKY WARBLER
Phylloscopus fuscatus

283. TWO-BARRED WARBLER
Phylloscopus plumbeitarsus

282. GREENISH WARBLER
Phylloscopus trochiloides

284. YELLOW-BELLIED WARBLER
Abroscopus superciliaris
L 4⅓". A bright olive-green bird with grey head and whitish eyebrow; throat and upper breast, white. Found in bamboo jungle and secondary growth up to 5,000 feet. Lively and active, and keeps in small parties. Breeds from March to June. Common resident.

GRASSBIRDS Megalurinae, Sylviidae
Two species of grassbird occur in Myanmar and both are resident.
Grassbirds are relatively large birds with long tails. They feed mainly on insects.

285. STRIATED GRASSBIRD
Megalurus palustris
L 10". A buff brown bird with broad black streaks on upper parts and rather long tail. Found in reedbeds, marshes and grassland; also in wet paddy fields, in river valleys and rushy swamps in the hills. Often sits on exposed perch. Pumps tail while in flight. Song consists of loud, rich, fluty warbling notes. Breeds from February to June. Common resident.

LAUGHINGTHRUSHES, Garrulacinae, Sylviidae
The laughingthrushes are represented in Myanmar by twenty-four species, and all are resident.

Laughingthrushes are stocky birds with strong bills, moderately long tails and horizontal body posture. They are gregarious, and clamber through the undergrowth with distinctive jerky movements, jumping from branch to branch abruptly or hopping on the ground in a somewhat clumsy fashion. They feed on beetles, insects, snails and leeches. Many species also take fruits, seeds and nectar.

286. WHITE-CRESTED LAUGHINGTHRUSH
Garrulax leucolophus
L 12". A bright rufous bird with white head, crest, throat and breast, and black band through eye. Found in thickets and undergrowth in forests and secondary growth of the foothills up to 4,000 feet. The most characteristic bird of teak forests. Sociable and keeps in small parties, more frequently in larger flocks. Unafraid of human habitation. Sings most strikingly in unison with brief low chattering followed by a chorus of diabolical cackling laughter, shattering the silence. Breeds from February to September. Common resident.

287. LESSER NECKLACED LAUGHINGTHRUSH
Garrulax moniliger
L 12". An olive-brown bird with black necklace and silvery white ear coverts, often without streaks; underparts, buff white; tail has black subterminal band. Found in undergrowth of forests and secondary growth up to 4,000 feet. Always in flocks, often mixed with other medium-sized species. Not very vocal; foraging flocks make a variety of low sounds. Breeds from March to May. Common resident.

288. GREATER NECKLACED LAUGHINGTHRUSH
Garrulax pectoralis
L 13". An olive-brown bird with black necklace and streaked ear coverts. Found in forests and secondary growth of the plains and foothills up to 4,000 feet. Always in flocks. Hops both on ground and from branch to branch. Flight rather clumsy. Very vocal with a strange, very human piping to which is usually added several short and high whistles, making a flock sound like an orchestra of mournful weepy piping; also grating noises. Breeds from March to May. Resident.

284. YELLOW-BELLIED WARBLER
Abroscopus superciliaris

285. STRIATED GRASSBIRD
Megalurus palustris

286. WHITE-CRESTED LAUGHINGTHRUSH
Garrulax leucolophus

287. LESSER NECKLACED LAUGHINGTHRUSH
Garrulax monileger

288. GREATER NECKLACED LAUGHINGTHRUSH
Garrulax pectoralis

289. CHESTNUT-CROWNED LAUGHINGTHRUSH
Garrulax erythrocephalus

L 10½". A dull-looking bird with very dark head and breast. Found in thick undergrowth in hill forests above 3,000 feet. Keeps in parties, feeding on or near the ground. Very shy and secretive. Feeds on insects and seeds on or near the ground. Call: variable, including *walk-to-work* or *too-rit-a-re-ill*. Breeds in April and May. Resident, except in C Myanmar.

290. RED-FACED LIOCICHLA
Liocichla phoenicea

L 9½". A brown bird with crimson sides of head and neck; wings, red-fringed with black and white marking; tail, blackish and orange-tipped. Found in undergrowth in evergreen forest, grass and scrub above 3,000 feet. Call: loud musical *chi-chweew chi-chweew chi-chweew*. Breeds from March to June. Resident in N, W, C and E Myanmar.

BABBLERS Timaliini, Sylviinae, Sylviidae

Myanmar has ninety-six species of babbler and all are resident.

Babblers are closely related to warblers and thrushes. They are poor fliers with short wings and a close soft plumage. They feed mainly on insects and go around in small flocks. Many of them chatter and make loud noises, but some have beautiful voices.

291. BUFF-BREASTED BABBLER
Pellorneum tickelli

L 6". A brown bird with whitish throat and abdomen; rest of underparts, buff. Found in undergrowth of dense evergreen and deciduous forests of the plains and lower hills. Skulks in dense undergrowth, partial to bamboo thickets near streams. Call: loud *pit-you pit-you*. Breeds from February to July. Resident.

292. PUFF-THROATED BABBLER
Pellorneum ruficeps

L 6½". A brown bird with rufous cap and streaked underparts. Found in forests in the plains and foothills, ascending locally to 5,000 feet. Goes about in small parties in bamboos and undergrowth, spending much of its life on ground, searching for insects. Sings persistently. Call: loud sweet *to-meet-you* or *pretty-dear*. Breeds from March to May. Common resident.

293. WHITE-BROWED SCIMITAR BABBLER
Pomatorhinus schisticeps

L 9". An olive-brown bird with pale yellowish bill. Found in forests, bamboo scrubs and grasslands up to 7,000 feet. Shy, seldom seen, but often heard. Lives on the ground or in thick cover close to the ground; ascends trees occasionally. Call: *kaw-kaw-ka-yit*. Breeds from March to May. Common resident.

294. STREAKED WREN BABBLER
Napothera brevicaudata

L 5–6¼". An olive-brown bird with rusty underparts; feathers of upper parts tipped with black; chin and throat, white with brown streaks. Found in moist and evergreen forests up to 7,000 feet. Favours rocky slopes. Keeps in pairs or small parties. Shy. Call: long shrill *pee-ee-oo* or *pee-oo*. Breeds from January to July. Resident, except in SW and C Myanmar.

289. CHESTNUT-CROWNED LAUGHINGTHRUSH
Garrulax erythrocephalus

290. RED-FACED LIOCICHLA
Liocichla phoenicea

291. BUFF-BREASTED BABBLER
Pellorneum tickelli

292. PUFF-THROATED BABBLER
Pellorneum ruficeps

293. WHITE-BROWED SCIMITAR BABBLER
Pomatorhinus schisticeps

294. STREAKED WREN BABBLER
Napothera brevicaudata

295. PYGMY WREN BABBLER
Pnoepyga pusilla
L 3½". A dark brown bird with white or rusty underparts. Found above 3,500 feet in undergrowth of higher hills. Usually solitary. Quiet and easily overlooked. Habitually opens and closes wings. Favours dense fern growth where it runs about like a small brown mouse. Song is a high-pitched *ti-ti-tu* repeated every 3–5 seconds. Breeds from April to June. Common resident, except in SW, C and S Myanmar.

296. RUFOUS-FRONTED BABBLER
Stachyris rufifrons
L 5". A small brown bird with rufous forehead and crown. Found in forests of the plains and foothills, ascending locally to 5,000 feet. Seen in small flocks, often mixed with other species, in undergrowth. Call: plaintive *peee peee peee peee peee*. Breeds from April to July. Not recorded in Chin Hills and N Myanmar. Resident.

297. GOLDEN BABBLER
Stachyris chrysaea
L 5". A bright golden-yellow bird with streaked crown. Found in dense undergrowth in higher hills above 3,000 feet. Partial to bamboo thickets. Occasionally ascends trees when feeding. Collects in large parties outside breeding season. Song is a low-pitched *sweep sweep sweep sweep sweep*. Breeds from April to July. Common resident, except in SW and C Myanmar.

298. GREY-THROATED BABBLER
Stachyris nigriceps
L 5½". A rather dark brown bird with streaked crown and whitish supercillium; throat, grey and underparts, rusty buff. Found in moist and evergreen forests up to 5,000 feet. Keeps in flocks, sometimes with other small babblers. Mostly remains hidden in thick underbrush. Call: *prrreee-prrreee*. Breeds from March to May. Resident.

299. STRIPED TIT-BABBLER
Macronous gularis
L 5¼". A brownish yellow bird with rufous crown and streaked throat and breast. Found in secondary growth, bamboo thickets and forests of the plains and foothills below 4,000 feet. A common and characteristic bird of teak forests. Active in dense vegetation in flocks of ten or more birds. Call: loud resonant choonk choonk choonk or tunk tunk tunk, also low hoarse *schwach-schwach* or *chrr-chrr*. Breeds from February to July. Common resident.

300. CHESTNUT-CAPPED BABBLER
Timalia pileata
L 7". An olive-brown bird with strong black bill and bright chestnut cap; prominent streaking on white throat. Found in bamboo thickets, secondary growth and tall grass up to 4,500 feet. Typically a bird of tall grass and similar vegetation in damp areas. Usually in small parties. Call: *chew-ayae*, chit chit chit chit or sometimes scree chit chit chit. Breeds from April to August. Common resident, mainly in low elevations.

301. YELLOW-EYED BABBLER
Chrysomma sinense
L 7½". A rufous brown bird with long tail and red orbital ring. Found in open country in scrub jungle, tall grass and clumps of bushes up to 6,000 feet. Often enters gardens. Usually in small parties. Strictly arboreal, but seldom flies. Seldom descends to the ground. Song is *twee-twee-ta-whit-chu* or *cheep cheep cheep cheep cheep*, alternating with kru-kru-kru. Breeds in July and August. Common resident, mainly in the plains.

295. PYGMY WREN BABBLER
Pnoepyga pusilla

296. RUFOUS-FRONTED BABBLER
Stachyris rufifrons

297. GOLDEN BABBLER
Stachyris chrysaea

298. GREY-THROATED BABBLER
Stachyris nigriceps

299. STRIPED TIT-BABBLER
Macronous gularis

300. CHESTNUT-CAPPED BABBLER
Timalia pileata

301. YELLOW-EYED BABBLER
Chrysomma sinense

302. STRIATED BABBLER
Turdoides earlei
L 9½". A light brown bird with streaked upper parts; chin, throat and breast, rufous with dark stripes. Found in extensive areas of marshes and tall grass in the plains. Always collects in noisy parties. Seldom descends to the ground. Feeds chiefly on insects. Call: *keep-quiet*. Breeds from March to October. Resident in SW, N, C and S Myanmar.

303. WHITE-THROATED BABBLER
Turdoides gularis
L 10". A common endemic species, familiar in towns and cities of C Myanmar; also in Ayeyarwaddy and Sittaung valleys, down to Yangon. Frequents hedges and thickets. Goes about in small parties, roving from hedge to hedge, from thorn bush to thorn bush in search of food. Call: grating, squeaky *cheep cheep* followed by a trill. Breeds from April to June.

304. SILVER-EARED MESIA
Leiothrix argentauris
L 7". A golden-yellow bird with black cap and silvery-white ear coverts. Found in scrub of higher hills above 3,000 feet. Often in large flocks of about thirty birds. Flits about in bushes in search of food. Not shy. Song is a cheery, slurred *wee-a-ree, woo-ee-oo, chee-ur-ee, che-wee-oo*. Breeds from April to July. Resident, except in SW and C Myanmar.

305. WHITE-BROWED SHRIKE BABBLER
Pteruthius flaviscapis
L 6½". Male: blackish with white eyebrow and whitish underparts. Female: greyish olive with whitish eyebrow and olive-green wings. Found in hill forests above 3,000 feet. Frequents all types of hill forests. A remarkably fearless bird. Slow in movements. Song is a loud musical *chuck-a-cheep* repeated two or three times. Breeds from April to June. Resident, except in SW Myanmar.

306. CHESTNUT-FRONTED SHRIKE BABBLER
Pteruthius aenobarbus
L 4½". Male: greenish-olive above, deep yellow below with white eyering and supercillium; forehead, chestnut; throat and upper breast, dark chestunt; two white bars on wing. Female: forehead, rufous; underparts, creamy white; wing-bars, pale rufous buff. Found in evergreen forest and edge above 4,000 feet. Solitary or paired, quietly hunting along low branches in deliberate fashion. Sings with various notes, repeated monotonously. Breeds from January to April. Resident, except in SW Myanmar.

307. WHITE-HOODED BABBLER
Gampsorhynchus rufulus
L 9½". A rufous brown bird with white head and pinkish bill. Found in bamboo thickets and undergrowth of evergreen forests, especially near water, up to 6,000 feet. Keeps entirely to trees, bushes and bamboo, not descending to the ground. Gregarious and not shy. Call: *kaw-ke-yawk*. Breeds from Apirl to August. Resident.

308. BLUE-WINGED MINLA
Minla cyanouroptera
L 6½". A dull brownish grey bird with white eyebrow and blue patches on wings and tail; underparts, white. Found in open evergreen and hill forests above 3,000 feet. Arboreal. Keeps in small parties. Call: *ter-ee-er-doo-der-di*. Breeds from December to June. Resident, except in SW, S and C Myanmar.

Birds of Myanmar

302. STRIATED BABBLER
Turdoides earlei

303. WHITE-THROATED BABBLER
Turdoides gularis

305. WHITE-BROWED SHRIKE BABBLER
Pteruthius flaviscapis

304. SILVER-EARED MESIA
Leiothrix argentauris

307. WHITE-HOODED BABBLER
Gampsorhynchus rufulus

306. CHESTNUT-FRONTED SHRIKE BABBLER
Pteruthius aenobarbus

308. BLUE-WINGED MINLA
Minla cyanouroptera

309. RUFOUS-WINGED FULVETTA
Alcippe castaneceps

L 4½". An olive-green bird with chestnut crown and nape; underparts, whitish. Found in evergreen forests above 3,500 feet. Usually in small parties. Keeps to low trees and bushes, often climbing on large tree trunks. Call: *tu-twee-twee*. Breeds from January to June. Resident, except in SW and C Myanmar.

310. BROWN-CHEEKED FULVETTA
Alcippe poioicephala

L 6½". An olive-brown bird with grey crown and nape. Found in forests of the foothills up to 4,500 feet. Frequents all types of forests, foraging through undergrowth and bamboo. Keeps in active, restless parties. Call: *chewy chewy chewy chewy chewy*. Breeds from January to September. Common resident.

311. RUFOUS-BACKED SIBIA
Heterophasia annectens

L 7⅔". A rufous bird with black head; nape, white-streaked; underparts, white; vent, buff. Found in evergreen forests above 3,000 feet. Favours treetops; often in undergrowth. Typically runs along branches, incessantly flirting tail. Usually silent. Song is a loud, strident *chwee chwee-chui, wi-wi-chi-chui* etc. Breeds from April to June. Resident, except in C and S Myanmar.

312. DARK-BACKED SIBIA
Heterophasia melanoleuca

L 9". A black bird with white underparts and long tail. Found in evergreen forest and adjacent scrub of higher hills above 3,000 feet. Arboreal and usually seen in treetops,often descending to undergrowth. Able to climb up tree trunks. Not shy, active in loose flocks. Song is a wavering *hrrrr'rrr'r'r'i-u, hrrrr'r'r'r'i-i* etc. Breeds from mid-February to early May. Common resident in north Tanintharyi, C and E Myanmar.

313. STRIATED YUHINA
Yuhina castaniceps

L 5½". A dull brown bird with short crest and faint white streaks on upper parts; ear and nape, chestnut. Found in lower canopy and top of undergrowth in the more open parts of hill forest at 2,000–6,000 feet. Usually seen in active parties. Call: a constant low *chir-chit chir-chit*. Breeds in April and May. Resident, locally common.

314. BURMESE YUHINA
Yuhina humilis

L 5". A brownish bird with short crest; upper parts, brown; underparts, white with fine brown streaks. An endemic resident species found in evergreen forests and secondary growth above 4,000 feet in a small range from Mt. Byingye (on the border between Yamethin District and the Southern Shan State) in the north to Mt. Mulayit in the south. Call: a low *chuck-chuck.....a chir chir chir chir..... chit-a-whit* repeated. Breeds in April.

315. WHITE-BELLIED YUHINA
Yuhina zantholeuca

L 5". A greenish-yellow bird with short erectile crest; underparts, white with bright yellow under tail coverts. Found in evergreen forests and secondary growth up to 6,000 feet (9,000 feet in N Myanmar) Frequents both undergrowth and treetops and partial to bamboo jungle. Normally silent and solitary, but occasionally collects in small parties. Song is a short *si'i'i'i'ii*. Breeds from February to June. Common resident.

309. RUFOUS-WINGED FULVETTA
Alcippe castaneceps

310. BROWN-CHEEKED FULVETTA
Alcippe poioicephala

311. RUFOUS-BACKED SIBIA
Heterophasia annectens

312. DARK-BACKED SIBIA
Heterophasia melanoleuca

313. STRIATED YUHINA
Yuhina castaniceps

314. BURMESE YUHINA
Yuhina humilis

315. WHITE-BELLIED YUHINA
Yuhina zantholeuca

316. GREY-HEADED PARROTBILL
Paradoxornis gularis

L 7½". A brownish bird with orange bill and silky white underparts. Found in ever-green forests, scrub and secondary growth at 2,000–6,000 feet. Seen in loose parties, and not shy. Usually silent. Call: *jiow-jiow* or *jieu jieu jieu*. Breeds from April to July. Resident in W, N and E Myanmar.

317. SPOT-BREASTED PARROTBILL
Paradoxornis guttaticollis

L 8". A pale brown bird with rufous cap, black ear coverts and chin and black-spotted throat and upper breast. Found in grassland and undergrowth above 3,000 feet. Keeps in small parties. Call: *twut twut twut twut twut twut twut*. Breeds from April to July. Resident in W, N and E Myanmar.

LARKS Alaudidae

Eight species of lark occur in Myanmar and six are resident.

Larks are terrestrial birds of open country with streaked, brownish plumage. They live in fields and meadows and feed on insects and seeds. They often sing while fluttering in the air. They build their nests on the ground. Sexes are alike.

318. BENGAL BUSHLARK
Mirafra assamica

L 6". A streaked, brownish bird with whitish throat. Found in open country, in paddy fields, grass and dry scrub jungle near cultivations below 2,000 feet. A characteristic bird of Dry Zone of C Myanmar. May appear in small groups. Feeds on ground. Perches on bushes and small trees. Call: *tzrep-tzi, tzee tzee tzee*. Breeds from April to October. Common resident in Tanintharyi, W, C and E Myanmar.

319. BURMESE BUSHLARK
Mirafra microptera

L 6". An endemic species. Found in bushes, scrub and cultivations. Mainly terrestrial, but often perches on trees; also on bushes and telephone wires. Call: b*eep beep beep, tsi tsi tsi tsi, tsupp tsupp tsupp*. Breeds from June to October. Resident in C and S (north) Myanmar.

320. SAND LARK
Calandrella raytal

L 5½". A pale sandy brown bird with finely streaked breast. Found on rivers, coastal sand and mudflats. A typical and extremely tame bird of the Ayeyarwaddy River, often observed scavenging among debris outside fishermen's huts. Call: *chrrru, chrrt chu, chirrru* etc. Breeds from mid-February to May. Resident in C and S Myanmar.

321. ORIENTAL SKYLARK
Alauda gulgula

L 6½". A streaked, brownish bird with a distinct crest. Found in open country, in paddy plains, grasslands, pastures and cultivations and on mudflats. Flight strong. Lives and feeds on the ground, picking up seeds, insects and fallen grains of rice. Call: *chizz-baz-baz, baz-terrr* etc. Breeds from March to July. Resident.

316. GREY-HEADED PARROTBILL
Paradoxornis gularis

317. SPOT-BREASTED PARROTBILL
Paradoxornis guttaticollis

318. BENGAL BUSHLARK
Mirafra assamica

319. BURMESE BUSHLARK
Mirafra microptera

320. SAND LARK
Calandrella raytal

321. ORIENTAL SKYLARK
Alauda gulgula

FLOWERPECKERS Dicaeini, Nectariniinae, Nectariniidae

The flowerpeckers are represented in Myanmar by ten species and all are resident.

Flowerpeckers are tiny birds with short bills and tails. Males are colourful, but females are duller. They live high up in treetops where they move about actively in small flocks among the branches. They feed on insects, nectar, berries and other soft fruits. They build hanging, purse-shaped nests suspended between twigs.

322. YELLOW-VENTED FLOWERPECKER
Dicaeum chrysorrheum

L 4". An olive-yellow bird with dark streaks on whitish underparts; primaries and tail, black; under tail coverts, bright yellow. Sexes alike. Found in open forests, secondary growth and gardens in plains and foothills, locally ascending to 5,000 feet. Call: *dzeep*. Breeds from May to August and December to January. Resident.

323. PLAIN FLOWERPECKER
Dicaeum concolor

L3⅔". A tiny olive-green bird with slightly decurved bill. Sexes alike. Found in forest, secondary growth and cultivations up to 4,000 feet. Keeps usually in pairs. Restless, showing off in presence of mate. Often seen on flowering trees, especially citrus. Sings with repeated, high-pitched *tsit tsi si si si si*. Breeds from March to August. Resident, except in S Myanmar.

324. FIRE-BREASTED FLOWERPECKER
Dicaeum ignipectus

L 31". Male: metallic blue-green upper parts and buff underparts with scarlet patch on breast. Female: olive-green above and buff below. Found in all types of hill forests above 2,000 feet. Keeps entirely to treetops. Song is a high-pitched, *strident see-bit see-bit see-bit see-bit*. Breeds from March to August. Resident, except in SW Myanmar.

325. SCARLET-BACKED FLOWERPECKER
Dicaeum cruentatum

L 3½". Male: crown, nape, back and upper tail coverts, red: sides of head, wings and tail, black. Female: grey brown above with red patch on rump. Found in secondary growth, scrub, cultivations and cities up to 4,000 feet. Partial to masses of parasitic plants that grow on trees. Usually seen in pairs or small parties. Bold and aggressive, sitting on exposed perch on top of trees or telephone wires. Song is a high-pitched *whee-ti-too-ti*. Breeds from March to June. Common resident.

SUNBIRDS, SPIDERHUNTERS Nectariniini, Nectariniinae, Nectariniidae

Myanmar has nineteen species of this group, and all are resident.

Sunbirds are tiny birds with long thin curved bills. Their tongues are long and almost tubular in structure and capable of extrusion beyond the bills. They feed on nectar and insects which they suck and eat by perching beside the flowers. In most species, males have metallic colours, whilst females are brown or greenish. When perched on a branch, they have a curious habit of stretching and contracting their necks rhythmically and at the same time swaying the body from side to side.

Spiderhunters are larger and more robust birds. Sexes are alike, and males lack bright metallic colours of sunbirds.

322. YELLOW-VENTED FLOWERPECKER
Dicaeum chrysorrheum

323. PLAIN FLOWERPECKER
Dicaeum concolor

324. FIRE-BREASTED FLOWERPECKER
Dicaeum ignipectus

325. SCARLET-BACKED FLOWERPECKER
Dicaeum cruentatum

326. OLIVE-BACKED SUNBIRD
Nectarinia jugularis

L 4½". Male: olive upper parts (not metallic) with metallic purple-black throat and yellow belly. Female: brown above and yellow below. Found in gardens and open forests below 3,000 feet. Feeds mainly on nectar. Call: *sweet*. Breeds from March to September. Resident, except in N Myanmar.

327. PURPLE SUNBIRD
Nectarinia asiatica

L 4½". Male: black with a metallic blue or purple gloss. Female: brown above and yellow below. Found in forests, gardens and cultivations of the plains and foothills, ascending to 5,000 feet. A typical bird of Dry Zone of C Myanmar, usually seen in parties. Not shy, often observed near human habitation. Call: *zit, swee* or *che-wee*. Breeds from February to May. Common resident.

328. MRS GOULD'S SUNBIRD
Aethopyga gouldiae

L 4⅓". (male tail up to 1¾" more). Male: crown, throat and tail, metallic blue; head, neck, mantle and breast, red; belly and rump, yellow. Female: olive-green with yellow belly and rump. Found in scrub and forests above 4,000 feet. Quite confiding. Call: *tzip tzip tzip tzip tzip, squeeee, tshi-stshi-ti-ti-ti*. Breeds from March to June. Resident.

329. CRIMSON SUNBIRD
Aethopyga siparaja

L 4½". (male tail 1" more). Male: mantle, throat and upper breast, crimson with elongated central tail feathers. Female: olive-green. Found in forests, secondary growth and cultivations throughout the plains and higher hills up to 4,500 feet. Feeds largely on insects. Call: *whit, tit, wit-it*. Breeds from January to July. Common resident.

330. LITTLE SPIDERHUNTER
Arachnothera longirostra

L 6⅓". An olive-green bird with long downcurved bill; throat, greyish white; belly and under tail coverts, yellow. Found in forest, secondary growth, gardens and cultivations up to 5,000 feet; favours banana groves. Solitary or paired. Active, but silent. Flight, surprisingly fast. Call: *itch* or *chit*. Breeds from December to October. Resident.

331. STREAKED SPIDERHUNTER
Arachnothera magna

L7½". A black-streaked spiderhunter with yellow legs. Found in forests and secondary growth up to 6,000 feet. Attracted to village gardens by flowering trees and shrubs. Fond of banana gardens. Active and noisy. Feeds on nectar, to some extent on insects and spiders. Call: *chit-ik* in flight. Breeds from April to August. Common resident.

SPARROWS, WAGTAILS, PIPITS, WEAVERS, MUNIAS Passeridae

Thirty-three species of this family occur in Myanmar and seventeen are resident.

Sparrows are familiar birds. Their conical bills are adapted to eating seeds and grains. Their tails are notched. They build loose, dome-shaped nests in holes or crevices or in the eaves of buildings.

Wagtails and pipits are slender terrestrial birds of the open country. They have pointed bills and long slender legs. They feed on insects, usually caught on the ground and occasionally snatched in the air. They are gregarious outside breeding season. Sexes are alike.

Wagtails are black and white or yellow in colour and have a long tail which is continuously wagged up and down.

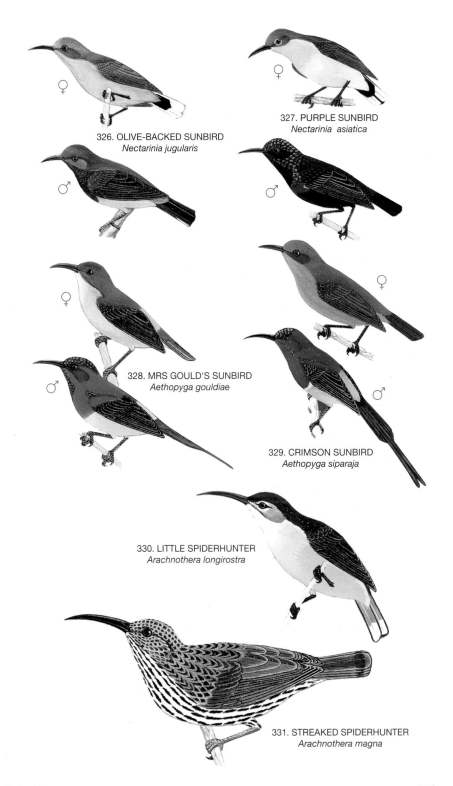

326. OLIVE-BACKED SUNBIRD
Nectarinia jugularis

327. PURPLE SUNBIRD
Nectarinia asiatica

328. MRS GOULD'S SUNBIRD
Aethopyga gouldiae

329. CRIMSON SUNBIRD
Aethopyga siparaja

330. LITTLE SPIDERHUNTER
Arachnothera longirostra

331. STREAKED SPIDERHUNTER
Arachnothera magna

Pipits are dull brownish with longitudinal stripes and shorter tails.

Weavers are similar to sparrows in shape and have slightlly rounded tails. They are birds of the paddy plains, open grasslands, cultivations and very open forests. They build elaborately woven nests, bag-shaped and suspended from outer branches of trees or beneath a palm, in colonies.

Munias are sparrow-like birds found in cultivations and grasslands, both in the plains and hills. They fly in close-packed flocks. They build globular nests with side entrances in bushes or tall grass.

332. HOUSE SPARROW
Passer domesticus
L 6". Male: grey crown and upper tail coverts. Female: pale rufous-white eyebrow and black streaks on back. Found in villages, cities, gardens and cultivations up to 4,000 feet. More rural and less urban than tree sparrow. Collects in large flocks in hot weather and rains. Call: *chirrup, chissick, chur-r-r-it-it-it*. Breeds year round. Common resident.

333. PLAIN-BACKED SPARROW
Passer flaveolus
L 5¾". Male: chestnut mantle and black throat. Female: light brown upper parts with buff eyebrow. Found in open country and cultivated clearings on the outskirts of forest below 5,000 feet. A rural species. Call: *filip* or *chirru*p. Breeds throughout the year. Endemic resident in W, C, S and E Myanmar.

334. EURASIAN TREE SPARROW
Passer montanus
L 5¾". Sexes similar with dark chestnut cap, white cheeks and black ear patch. Found in villages, cities, gardens, and cultivations up to 6,000 feet. It is the real "house sparrow" over most parts of the country. Nests under the eaves and roofs of buldings or in holes in trees and walls. Call: *chip, chissip, tet, tsooit*. Breeds year round, mainly from May to August. Common resident, mostly in lowlands.

335. WHITE WAGTAIL
Motacilla alba
L 7½". A pied wagtail with white underparts and large white patch on wing coverts. Found in open country up to 6500 feet, often near water. Terrestrial and walks about on ground, incessantly wagging long tail up and down. Perches on bridges and culverts, but not on trees. Call: *tsli-vitt*. Migrant. (Two races, leucopsis and alboides, have been known to breed in N Myanmar.)

336. GREY WAGTAIL
Motacilla cinerea
L 7½". A grey and yellow bird with blackish wing coverts. Found in plains and open forests, near flowing streams; favours damp, gritty sand gravel. A characteristic bird of jungle streams of teak forests in Bago Yoma in cold season. Solitary. Call: *tittick* or *tzit-tzit*. Winter visitor, August to April.

337. RICHARD'S PIPIT
Anthus richardi
L 6–8". A streaked tawny-brown bird with a markedly long hind claw. Found in open country in cultivations, paddy fields, grazing grounds and golf courses up to 6,000 feet. Frequently hovers before landing. Typically adopts upright posture. Call: *schree-ep* or *shreep* in flight. Breeds from March to August. Common resident.

332. HOUSE SPARROW
Passer domesticus

♀

♂

♀

♂

333. PLAIN-BACKED SPARROW
Passer flaveolus

♀

334. EURASIAN TREE SPARROW
Passer montanus

335. WHITE WAGTAIL
Motacilla alba

♂

337. RICHARD'S PIPIT
Anthus richardi

336. GREY WAGTAIL
Motacilla cinerea

338. PADDYFIELD PIPIT
Anthus rufulus

L 6½". A streaked tawny-brown bird, similar to, but much smaller than, Richard's Pipit. Found in open areas and drier cultivations up to 5,000 feet. Feeds on the ground. Perches on bushes, but never in trees during breeding season. Call: *chip, chup* or *chwist*, usually in flight. Breeds from January to August. Resident.

339. OLIVE-BACKED PIPIT
Anthus hodgsoni

L 6½". A brownish olive-green bird with white eyebrow and bold blackish streaks on breast. Found in forest, secondary growth and wooded areas up to 8,500 feet. Secretive. Often found walking amongst undergrowth and leaf-litter. Perches in trees. Call: *teez* or *spiz* in flight. Resident in W and N Myanmar and migrant over rest of the country.

340. STREAKED WEAVER
Ploceus manyar

L 5½". Male: yellow cap and blackish face. Female: yellowish eyebrow and boldly streaked throat and breast. Male similar to female outside breeding season. Found in grass, secondary growth and cultivations below 3,000 feet. Call: *chirt*. Breeds during the rains. Resident, except in Tanintharyi.

341. BAYA WEAVER
Ploceus philippinus

L 6". Male: yellow cap which he loses in winter. Female: unstreaked or faintly streaked underparts. Found in secondary growth, cultivations and paddy fields throughout the plains and foothills, ascending to 4,000 feet. Usually in large flocks. Feeds on seeds and insects. Call: *chit chit chit*. Breeds during the rains. Common resident, abundant in the plains.

342. ASIAN GOLDEN WEAVER
Ploceus hypoxanthus

L 6". Male: yellowish with black mask and throat. Female: tawny eyebrow with unstreaked underparts. Male similar to female outside breeding season. Found in secondary growth and cultivations of lower elevations. Usually seen in vegetation growing in water or swamps. Call: *chit chit chit*. Breeds during the rains. Resident, except in N and E Myanmar.

343. RED AVADAVAT
Amandava amandava

L 4". Brown above and buff brown below with red bill and upper tail coverts, and white spots on wings. Male in breeding plumage is bright red with white spots on underparts. Found in reeds and grasses of damp and well-wooded localities. Gregarious. Call: thin *pseep, teei* or *tsi*, particularly in flight. Breeds from January to September. Resident, except in Tanintharyi.

344. WHITE-RUMPED MUNIA
Lonchura striata

L 4½". Blackish brown plumage with white rump, buff white belly and pointed black tail. Sexes alike. Found in paddy fields, cultivations, scrub and second grwoth. Gregarious. Flight even and direct, but unsustained. Common in paddy fields and taungyas of forest villages. Attracted into forests by seeding bamboos. Call: trilled *prrri*t. Breeds all year. Resident.

338. PADDYFIELD PIPIT
Anthus rufulus

339. OLIVE-BACKED PIPIT
Anthus hodgsoni

♀

♀

340. STREAKED WEAVER
Ploceus manyar

♂

341. BAYA WEAVER
Ploceus philippinus

♂

♀

♂

343. RED AVADAVAT
Amandava amandava

♀

♂

342. ASIAN GOLDEN WEAVER
Ploceus hypoxanthus

344. WHITE-RUMPED MUNIA
Lonchura striata

Birds of Myanmar

345. SCALY-BREASTED MUNIA
Lonchura punctulata

L 4½". Pale brown plumage with bold scaling on breast and flanks. Sexes alike. Found in grass, scrub, gardens, paddy fields and secondary growth throughout the plains and foothills, ascending to 5,000 feet. A familiar garden bird, and more of a Dry Zone bird than other munias. Often nests communally in houses. Call: *ki-dee ki-dee*. Breeds during the rains, but eggs laid as late as December. Common resident.

346. BLACK-HEADED MUNIA
Lonchura malacca

L 4½". Light chestnut plumage with black head, throat and upper breast. Sexes alike. Found in grass, scrub, reedbeds, marshes and secondary growth throughout the plains and foothills, ascending to 5,000 feet. Sociable. Call: weak, *reedy pee, pee*. Breeds during the rains, mostly in July and August. Resident.

FINCHES, BUNTINGS Fringillidae

This family is represented in Myanmar by twenty-nine species, of which fifteen are resident.

Finches and buntings are small to medium-sized birds with thick conical bills and notched tails. Males are colourful, and females are usually dull. They live in open country in grass and forest edge and feed primarily on seeds. They move about in flocks outside breeding season.

347. BLACK-HEADED GREENFINCH
Carduelis ambigua

L 5½". Male: head, wings and tail, blackish; underparts, yellow with olive streaks. Female: duller and browner with grey-green head. Found in open hill forests or open fields dotted with trees above 4,000 feet. Arboreal, favours treetops. Song is a continuous *scree* or *treeee-tertra*h. Breeds from July to October. Resident in W, N and E Myanmar.

348. COMMON ROSEFINCH
Carpodacus erythrinus

L 6½". Male: crimson plumage with browner upper parts and white or rosy lower belly and under tail coverts. Female: greyish-brown above, whitish below with dark streaks on throat, breast and upper abdomen. Found in open forest, scrub and cultivations in the hills and plains. Usually in small parties. Feeds mostly on ground, also on flowering trees. Call: soft *twee-eck*. Winter visitor.

349. CRESTED BUNTING
Melophus lathami

L 6½". A dark bird with long, pointed crest and rufous wings and tail; male is black; female, olive brown. Found in rocky slopes and hillside cultivations. Active and bold. Feeds on ground, picking up grass seeds; also hawks flies and flying ants. Call: *tweet-twe-twe-too*. Breeds from Apirl to August. Resident.

350. LITTLE BUNTING
Emberiza pusilla

L 5". A small streaked bird with rufous sides of head. Sexes alike. Found in grass, scrub and cultivations. Gregarious. Call: high, quiet pwick. Winter visitor, October to April, in enormous numbers to higher hills of N Myanmar; fairly common in C Myanmar.

345. SCALY-BREASTED MUNIA
Lonchura punctulata

346. BLACK-HEADED MUNIA
Lonchura malacca

♀

347. BLACK-HEADED GREENFINCH
Carduelis ambigua

♀

♂

348. COMMON ROSEFINCH
Carpodacus erythrinus

♂

350. LITTLE BUNTING
Emberiza pusilla

♂

349. CRESTED BUNTING
Melophus lathami

♀

Check-List of the Birds of Myanmar

Definitions:

r = Former resident, current status unknown
R = Resident
W = Winter visitor
V = Vagrant
? = Recorded, current status uncertain/
formerly occured status unclear
M = Migrant
P = Passage
B = Breeding visitor
w = Former winter visitor, current status
unknown
NB = Non-breeding visitor
nb = Former non-breeding visitor, current status
uncertain

MEGAPODIIDAE: Scrubfowl

1. NICOBAR SCRUBFOWL
    (Megapodius nicobariensis) (r)

PHASIANIDAE: Francolins, partridges, quails, pheasants & junglefowl

2. CHINESE FRANCOLIN
    (Francolinus pintadeanus) (R)
3. LONG-BILLED PARTRIDGE
    (Rhizothera longirostris) (R)
4. COMMON QUAIL *(Coturnix coturnix)* (W/V)
5. JAPANESE QUAIL *(Coturnix japonica)* (W)
6. RAIN QUAIL *(Coturnix coromandelica)* (R)
7. BLUE-BREASTED QUAIL *(Coturnix chinensis)* (R)
8. HILL PARTRIDGE *(Arborophila torqueola)* (R)
9. RUFOUS-THROATED PARTRIDGE
    (Arborophila rufogularis) (R)
10. WHITE-CHEEKED PARTRIDGE
    (Arborophila atrogularis) (R)
11. BAR-BACKED PARTRIDGE
    (Arborophila brunneopectus) (R)
12. SCALY-BREASTED PARTRIDGE *(Arboraphila chloropus)* (R)
13. CHESTNUT-NECKLACED PARTRIDGE
    (Arborophila charltonii) (R)
14. FERRUGINOUS PARTRIDGE *(Caloperdix oculea)* (R)
15. CRESTED PARTRIDGE *(Rollulus rouloul)* (R)
16. MOUNTAIN BAMBOO PARTRIDGE
    (Bambusicola fytchii) (R)
17. BLOOD PHEASANT *(Ithaginis cruentus)* (R)
18. BLYTH'S TRAGOPAN *(Tragopan blythii)* (R)
19. TEMMINCK'S TRAGOPAN
    (Tragopan temminckii) (R)
20. HIMALAYAN MONAL *(Lophophorus impejanus)* (R)
21. SCLATER'S MONAL *(Lophophorus sclateri)* (R)
22. RED JUNGLEFOWL *(Gallus gallus)* (R)

23. KALIJ PHEASANT *(Lophura leucomelanos)* (R)
24. SILVER PHEASANT *(Lophura nycthemera)* (R)
25. CRESTED FIREBACK *(Lophura ignita)* (R)
26. MRS HUME'S PHEASANT
    (Syrmaticus humiae) (R)
27. COMMON PHEASANT *(Phasianus colchicus)* (R)
28. LADY AMHERST'S PHEASANT
    (Chrysolophus amherstiae) (R)
29. GREY PEACOCK PHEASANT
    (Polyplectron bicalcaratum) (R)
30. MALAYAN PEACOCK PHEASANT
    (Polyplectron malacense) (R)
31. GREAT ARGUS *(Argusianus argus)* (R)
32. GREEN PEAFOWL *(Pavo muticus)* (R/r)

DENDROCYGNIDAE: Whistling-ducks

33. FULVOUS WHISTLING-DUCK
    (Dendrocygna bicolor) (R/r/?)
34. LESSER WHISTLING DUCK
    (Dendrocygna javanica) (R)

ANATIDAE: Anatinae:
Anserini: Geese, atypical ducks & pygmy-geese

35. BEAN GOOSE *(Anser fabalis)* (V)
36. GREATER WHITE- FRONTED GOOSE
    (Anser albifrons) (V)
37. LESSER WHITE-FRONTED GOOSE
    (Anser erythropus) (V)
38. GREYLAG GOOSE *(Anser anser)* (W)
39. BAR-HEADED GOOSE *(Anser indicus)* (W/V)
40. RUDDY SHELDUCK *(Tadorna ferruginea)* (W)
41. COMMON SHELDUCK *(Tadorna tadorna)* (V)
42. WHITE-WINGED DUCK *(Cairina scutulata)* (R/r)
43. COMB DUCK *(Sarkidiornis melanotos)* (R)
44. COTTON PYGMY-GOOSE
    (Nettapus coromandelianus) (R)

Anatini: Typical ducks

45. MANDARIN DUCK *(Aix galericulata)* (V)
46. GADWALL *(Anas strepera)* (W)
47. FALCATED DUCK *(Anas falcata)* (W/M)
48. EURASIAN WIGEON *(Anas penelope)* (W)
49. MALLARD *(Anas platyrhynchos)* (W)
50. SPOT-BILLED DUCK *(Anas poecilorhyncha)* (R)
51. NORTHERN SHOVELER *(Anas clypeata)* (W)
52. SUNDA TEAL *(Anas gibberifrons)* (?/V)
53. NORTHERN PINTAIL *(Anas acuta)* (W)
54. GARGANEY *(Anas querquedula)* (W)
55. BAIKAL TEAL *(Anas formosa)* (?)
56. COMMON TEAL *(Anas crecca)* (W)
57. PINK-HEADED DUCK
    (Rhodonessa caryophyllacea) (?)

58. RED-CRESTED POCHARD *(Rhodonessa rufina)* (W)
59. COMMON POCHARD *(Aythya ferina)* (W)
60. FERRUGINOUS POCHARD *(Aythya nyroca)* (W)
61. BAER'S POCHARD *(Aythya baeri)* (W)
62. TUFTED DUCK *(Aythya fuligula)* (W)
63. GREATER SCAUP *(Aythya marila)* (V)
64. COMMON GOLDENEYE *(Bucephala clangula)* (V)
65. SMEW *(Mergellus albellus)* (V)
66. COMMON MERGANSER *(Mergus merganser)* (W)

TURNICIDAE : Buttonquails

67. SMALL BUTTONQUAIL *(Turnix sylvatica)* (R)
68. YELLOW-LEGGED BUTTONQUAIL *(Turnix tanki)* (R)
69. BARRED BUTTONQUAIL *(Turnix suscitator)* (R)

INDICATORIDAE: Honeyguides

70. YELLOW-RUMPED HONEYGUIDE *(Indicator xanthonotus)* (R)

PICIDAE: Wrynecks, piculets & typical woodpeckers

71. EURASIAN WRYNECK *(Jynx torquilla)* (W/P)
72. SPECKLED PICULET *(Picumnus innominatus)* (R)
73. RUFOUS PICULET *(Sasia abnormis)* (R)
74. WHITE-BROWED PICULET *(Sasia ochracea)* (R)
75. GREY-CAPPED Woodpecker *(Dendrocopos canicapillus)* (R)
76. FULVOUS-BREASTED Woodpecker *(Dendrocopos macei)* (R)
77. STRIPE-BREASTED WOODPECKER *(Dendrocopos atratus)* (R)
78. YELLOW-CROWNED WOODPECKER *(Dendrocopos mahrattensis)* (R)
79. RUFOUS-BELLIED WOODPECKER *(Dendrocops hyperythrus)* (R)
80. CRIMSON-BREASTED WOODPECKER *(Dendrocopos cathpharius)* (R)
81. DARJEELING WOODPECKER *(Dendrocopos darjellensis)* (R)
82. GREAT SPOTTED WOODPECKER *(Dendrocopos major)* (R)
83. RUFOUS Woodpecker *(Celeus brachyurus)* (R)
84. WHITE-BELLIED WOODPECKER *(Dryocopus javensis)* (R)
85. BANDED WOODPECKER *(Picus miniaceus)* (R)
86. LESSER YELLOWNAPE *(Picus chlorolophus)* (R)
87. CRIMSON-WINGED WOODPECKER *(Picus puniceus)* (R)
88. GREATER YELLOWNAPE *(Picus flavinucha)* (R)
89. CHECKER-THROATED Woodpecker *(Picus mentalis)* (R)
90. STREAK-BREASTED WOODPECKER *(Picus viridanus)* (R)
91. LACED WOODPECKER *(Picus vittatus)* (R)

92. STREAK-THROATED WOODPECKER *(Picus xanthopygaeus)* (R)
93. BLACK-HEADED WOODPECKER *(Picus erythropygius)* (R)
94. GREY-HEADED WOODPECKER *(Picus canus)* (R)
95. OLIVE-BACKED WOODPECKER *(Dinopium rafflesii)* (R)
96. HIMALAYAN FLAMEBACK *(Dinopium shorii)* (R)
97. COMMON FLAMEBACK *(Dinopium javanense)* (R)
98. BLACK-RUMPED FLAMEBACK *(Dinopium benghalense)* (R)
99. GREATER FLAMEBACK *(Chrysocolaptes lucidus)* (R)
100. PALE-HEADED WOODPECKER *(Gecinulus grantia)* (R)
101. BAMBOO WOODPECKER *(Gecinulus viridis)* (R)
102. MAROON WOODPECKER *(Blythipicus rubiginosus)* (R)
103. BAY WOODPECKER *(Blythipicus pyrrhotis)* (R)
104. BUFF-RUMPED WOODPECKER *(Meiglyptes tristis)* (R)
105. BLACK-AND-BUFF WOODPECKER *(Meiglyptes jugularis)* (R)
106. BUFF-NECKED WOODPECKER *(Meiglyptes tukki)* (R)
107. GREY-AND-BUFF WOODPECKER *(Hemicircus concretus)* (R)
108. HEART-SPOTTED WOODPECKER *(Hemicircus canente)* (R)
109. GREAT SLATY WOODPECKER *(Mulleripicus pulverulentus)* (R)

MEGALAIMIDAE: Asian barbets

110. GREAT BARBET *(Megalaima virens)* (R)
111. LINEATED BARBET *(Megalaima lineata)* (R)
112. RED-CROWNED BARBET *(Megalaima rafflesii)* (R)
113. RED-THROATED BARBET *(Megalaima mystacophanos)* (R)
114. GOLDEN-THROATED BARBET *(Megalaima franklinii)* (R)
115. BLUE-THROATED BARBET *(Megalaima asiatica)* (R)
116. MOUSTACHED BARBET *(Megalaima incognita)* (R)
117. BLUE-EARED BARBET *(Megalaima australis)* (R)
118. COPPERSMITH BARBET *(Megalaima haemacephala)* (R)
119. BROWN BARBET *(Calorhamphus fuliginosus)* (R)

BUCEROTIDAE: Asian hornbills

120. ORIENTAL PIED HORNBILL *(Anthracoceros albirostris)* (R)

121. GREAT HORNBILL *(Buceros bicornis)* (R)
122. HELMETED HORNBILL *(Buceros vigil)* (R)
123. BROWN HORNBILL *(Anorrhinus tickelli)* (R)
124. BUSHY-CRESTED HORNBILL *(Anorrhinus galeritus)* (R)
125. WHITE-CROWNED HORNBILL *(Aceros comatus)* (R)
126. RUFOUS-NECKED HORNBILL *(Aceros nipalensis)* (R)
127. WREATHED HORNBILL *(Aceros undulatus)* (R)
128. PLAIN-POUCHED HORNBILL *(Aceros subruficollis)* (R)

UPUPIDAE: Hoopoes

129. COMMON HOOPOE *(Upupa epops)* (R/W)

TROGONIDAE: Harpactini: Asian trogons

130. SCARLET- RUMPED TROGON *(Harpactes duvaucelii)* (R)
131. ORANGE-BREASTED TROGON *(Harpactes oreskios)* (R)
132. RED-HEADED TROGON *(Harpactes erythrocephalus)* (R)
133. WARD'S TROGON *(Harpactes wardi)* (R)

CORACIIDAE: Rollers

134. INDIAN ROLLER *(Coracias benghalensis)* (R)
135. DOLLARBIRD *(Eurystomus orientalis)* (R)

ALCEDINIDAE: Smaller kingfishers

136. BLYTH'S KINGFISHER *(Alcedo hercules)* (R)
137. COMMON KINGFISHER *(Alcedo atthis)* (R/W)
138. BLUE-EARED KINGFISHER *(Alcedo meninting)* (R)
139. BLUE-BANDED KINGFISHER *(Alcedo euryzona)* (R)
140. BLACK-BACKED KINGFISHER *(Ceyx erithacus)* (R/P)

HALCYONIDAE: Larger kingfishers

141. BANDED KINGFISHER *(Lacedo pulchella)* (R)
142. BROWN-WINGED KINGFISHER *(Halcyon amauroptera)* (R)
143. STORK-BILLED KINGFISHER *(Halcyon capensis)* (R)
144. RUDDY KINGFISHER *(Halcyon coromanda)* (?)
145. WHITE-THROATED KINGFISHER *(Halcyon smyrnensis)* (R)
146. BLACK-CAPPED KINGFISHER *(Halcyon pileata)* (R or B/W)
147. COLLARED KINGFISHER *(Todiramphus chloris)* (R)
148. RUFOUS-COLLARED KINGFISHER *(Actenoides concretus)* (R)

CERYLIDAE: Pied kingfishers

149. CRESTED KINGFISHER *(Megaceryle lugubris)* (R)
150. PIED KINGFISHER *(Ceryle rudis)* (R)

MEROPIDAE: Bee-eaters

151. RED-BEARDED BEE-EATER *(Nyctyornis amictus)* (R)
152. BLUE-BEARDED BEE-EATER *(Nyctyornis athertoni)* (R)
153. GREEN BEE-EATER *(Merops orientalis)* (R)
154. BLUE-TAILED BEE-EATER *(Merops philippinus)* (R/B/W/P)
155. CHESTNUT-HEADED BEE-EATER *(Merops leschenaulti)* (R)

CUCULIDAE: Old World cuckoos

156. PIED CUCKOO *(Clamator jacobinus)* (B)
157. CHESTNUT-WINGED CUCKOO *(Clamator coromandus)* (B/B or R/?)
158. LARGE HAWK CUCKOO *(Hierococcyx sparverioides)* (R/?)
159. COMMON HAWK CUCKOO *(Hierococcyx varius)* (R)
160. MOUSTACHED HAWK CUCKOO *(Hierococcyx vagans)* (R)
161. HODGSON'S HAWK CUCKOO *(Hierococcyx fugax)* (R)
162. INDIAN CUCKOO *(Cuculus micropterus)* (R)
163. EURASIAN CUCKOO *(Cuculus canorus)* (B/P/?)
164. ORIENTAL CUCKOO *(Cuculus saturatus)* (B/W/P)
165. LESSER CUCKOO *(Cuculus poliocephalus)* (B/P/?)
166. BANDED BAY CUCKOO *(Cacomantis sonneratii)* (R)
167. GREY-BELLIED CUCKOO *(Cacomantis passerinus)* (?)
168. PLAINTIVE CUCKOO *(Cacomantis merulinus)* (R)
169. ASIAN EMERALD CUCKOO *(Chrysococcyx maculatus)*(R)
170. VIOLET CUCKOO *(Chrysococcyx xanthorhynchus)* (R)
171. DRONGO CUCKOO *(Surniculus lugubris)* (R)
172. ASIAN KOEL *(Eudynamys scolopacea)* (R)
173. BLACK-BELLIED MALKOHA *(Phaenicophaeus diardi)* (R)
174. CHESTNUT-BELLIED MALKOHA *(Phaenicophaeus sumatranus)* (R)
175. GREEN-BILLED MALKOHA *(Phaenicophaeus tristis)* (R)
176. RAFFLES'S MALKOHA *(Phaenicophaeus chlorophaeus)* (R)
177. RED-BILLED MALKOHA *(Phaenicophaeus javanicus)* (R)

178. CHESTNUT-BREASTED MALKOHA *(Phaenicophaeus curvirostris)* (R)

CENTROPODIDAE: Coucals

179. GREATER COUCAL *(Centropus sinensis)* (R)
180. BROWN COUCAL *(Centropus andamanensis)* (R)
181. LESSER COUCAL *(Centropus bengalensis)* (R)

PSITTACIDAE: Parrots & parakeets

182. BLUE-RUMPED PARROT *(Psittinus cyanurus)* (R)
183. VERNAL HANGING PARROT *(Loriculus vernalis)* (R)
184. ALEXANDRINE PARAKEET *(Psittacula eupatria)* (R)
185. ROSE-RINGED PARAKEET *(Psittacula krameri)* (R)
186. GREY-HEADED PARAKEET *(Psittacula finschii)* (R)
187. BLOSSOM-HEADED PARAKEET *(Psittacula roseata)* (R)
188. RED-BREASTED PARAKEET *(Psittacula alexandri)* (R)
189. LONG-TAILED PARAKEET *(Psittacula longicauda)* (R)

APODIDAE: Swifts

190. GLOSSY SWIFTLET *(Collocalia esculenta)* (R)
191. HIMALAYAN SWIFTLET *(Collocalia brevirostris)* (R/?)
192. BLACK-NEST SWIFTLET *(Collocalia maxima)* (R)
193. EDIBLE-NEST SWIFTLET *(Collocalia fuciphaga)* (V or offshore B)
194. GERMAIN'S SWIFTLET *(Collocalia germani)* (R)
195. SILVER-RUMPED NEEDLETAIL *(Rhaphidura leucopygialis)* (R)
196. WHITE-THROATED NEEDLETAIL *(Hirundapus caudacutus)* (?)
197. SILVER-BACKED NEEDLETAIL *(Hirundapus cochinchinensis)* (?)
198. BROWN-BACKED NEEDLETAIL *(Hirundapus giganteus)* (R)
199. ASIAN PALM SWIFT *(Cypsiurus balasiensis)* (R)
200. FORK-TAILED SWIFT *(Apus pacificus)* (R/?)
201. HOUSE SWIFT *(Apus affinis)* (R/?)
202. ALPINE SWIFT *(Apus melba)* (?)

HEMIPROCNIDAE: Treeswifts

203. CRESTED TREESWIFT *(Hemiprocne coronata)* (R)
204. GREY-RUMPED TREESWIFT *(Hemiprocne longipennis)* (R)
205. WHISKERED TREESWIFT *(Hemiprocne comata)* (R)

TYTONIDAE: Barn, grass and bay owls

206. BARN OWL *(Tyto alba)* (R)
207. GRASS OWL *(Tyto capensis)* (R)
208. ORIENTAL BAY OWL *(Phodilus badius)* (R)

STRIGIDAE: Typical owls

209. WHITE-FRONTED SCOPS OWL *(Otus sagittatus)* (R)
210. MOUNTAIN SCOPS OWL *(Otus spilocephalus)* (R)
211. ORIENTAL SCOPS OWL *(Otus sunia)* (R/W)
212. COLLARED SCOPS OWL *(Otus bakkamoena)* (R)
213. EURASIAN EAGLE OWL *(Bubo bubo)* (?)
214. SPOT-BELLIED EAGLE OWL *(Bubo nipalensis)* (R)
215. BARRED EAGLE OWL *(Bubo sumatranus)* (R)
216. DUSKY EAGLE OWL *(Bubo coromandus)* (R)
217. BROWN FISH OWL *(Ketupa zeylonensis)* (R)
218. TAWNY FISH OWL *(Ketupa flavipes)* (R)
219. BUFFY FISH OWL *(Ketupa ketupa)* (R)
220. SPOTTED WOOD OWL *(Strix seloputo)* (R)
221. MOTTLED WOOD OWL *(Strix ocellata)* (R)
222. BROWN WOOD OWL *(Strix leptogrammica)* (R)
223. TAWNY OWL *(Strix aluco)* (R)
224. COLLARED OWLET *(Glaucidium brodiei)* (R)
225. ASIAN BARRED OWLET *(Glaucidium cuculoides)* (R)
226. JUNGLE OWLET *(Glaucidium radiatum)* (R)
227. SPOTTED OWLET *(Athene brama)* (R)
228. BROWN HAWK OWL *(Ninox scutulata)* (R)
229. LONG-EARED OWL *(Asio otus)* (V)
230. SHORT-EARED OWL *(Asio flammeus)* (W)

BATRACHOSTOMIDAE: Asian frogmouths

231. HODGSON'S FROGMOUTH *(Batrachostomus hodgsoni)* (R)
232. JAVAN FROGMOUTH *(Batrachostomus javensis)* (R)

EUROSTOPODIDAE: Eared nightjars

233. GREAT EARED NIGHTJAR *(Eurostopodus macrotis)* (R)

CAPRIMULGIDAE:
Caprimulginae: Typical nighjars

234. GREY NIGHTJAR *(Caprimulgus indicus)* (R/W)
235. LARGE-TAILED NIGHTJAR *(Caprimulgus macrurus)* (R)
236. INDIAN NIGHTJAR *(Caprimulgus asiaticus)* (R)
237. SAVANNA NIGHTJAR *(Caprimulgus affinis)* (R)

COLUMBIDAE: Pigeons & doves

238. ROCK PIGEON *(Columba livia)* (R)
239. SNOW PIGEON *(Columba leuconota)*
    (Possibly R)
240. SPECKLED WOOD PIGEON *(Columba hodgsonii)* (R)
241. ASHY WOOD PIGEON *(Columba pulchricollis)* (R)
242. PALE-CAPPED PIGEON *(Columba punicea)* (R)
243. ORIENTAL TURTLE DOVE *(Streptopelia orientalis)* (R/W)
244. SPOTTED DOVE *(Streptopelia chinensis)* (R)
245. RED COLLARED DOVE *(Streptopelia tranquebarica)* (R)
246. EURASIAN COLLARED DOVE *(Streptopelia decaocto)* (R)
247. BARRED CUCKOO DOVE *(Macropygia unchall)* (R)
248. LITTLE CUCKOO DOVE *(Macropygia ruficeps)* (R)
249. EMERALD DOVE *(Chalcophaps indica)* (R)
250. PEACEFUL DOVE *(Geopelia striata)* (R)
251. NICOBAR PIGEON *(Caloenas nicobarica)* (R)
252. CINNAMON-HEADED GREEN PIGEON *(Treron fulvicollis)* (R)
253. PINK-NECKED GREEN PIGEON *(Treron vernans)* (R)
254. ORANGE-BREASTED GREEN PIGEON *(Treron bicincta)* (R)
255. POMPADOUR GREEN PIGEON *(Treron pompadora)* (R)
256. THICK-BILLED GREEN PIGEON *(Treron curvirostra)* (R)
257. LARGE GREEN PIGEON *(Treron capellei)* (R)
258. YELLOW-FOOTED GREEN PIGEON *(Treron phoenicoptera)* (R)
259. PIN-TAILED GREEN PIGEON *(Treron apicauda)* (R)
260. WEDGE-TAILED GREEN PIGEON *(Treron sphenura)* (R)
261. GREEN IMPERIAL PIGEON *(Ducula aenea)* (R)
262. MOUNTAIN IMPERIAL PIGEON *(Ducula badia)* (R)
263. PIED IMPERIAL PIGEON *(Ducula bicolor)* (R/?)

OTIDIDAE: Bustards

264. GREAT BUSTARD *(Otis tarda)* (V)

GRUIDAE:
Gruinae: Typical cranes

265. SARUS CRANE *(Grus antigone)* (R/r/?)
266. DEMOISELLE CRANE *(Grus virgo)* (V)
267. COMMON CRANE *(Grus grus)* (W/?)

HELIORNITHIDAE: Finfoots

268. MASKED FINFOOT *(Heliopais personata)* (R/?)

RALLIDAE: Rails, gallinules & coots

269. RED-LEGGED CRAKE *(Rallina fasciata)* (P/?)
270. SLATY-LEGGED CRAKE *(Rallina eurizonoides)* (?)
271. SLATY-BREASTED RAIL *(Gallirallus striatus)* (R)
272. WATER RAIL *(Rallus aquaticus)* (W)
273. WHITE-BREASTED WATERHEN *(Amaurornis phoenicurus)* (R)
274. BROWN CRAKE *(Porzana akool)* (R)
275. BLACK-TAILED CRAKE *(Porzana bicolor)* (R)
276. BAILLON'S CRAKE *(Porzana pusilla)* (W)
277. SPOTTED CRAKE *(Porzana porzana)* (V)
278. RUDDY-BREASTED CRAKE *(Porzana fusca)* (R/W)
279. WATERCOCK *(Gallicrex cinerea)* (R/B/?)
280. PURPLE SWAMPHEN *(Porphyrio porphyrio)* (R)
281. COMMON MOORHEN *(Gallinula chloropus)* (R/W)
282. COMMON COOT *(Fulica atra)* (W)

SCOLOPACIDAE:
Scolopacinae: Woodcocks & snipes

283. EURASIAN WOODCOCK *(Scolopax rusticola)* (R/W)
284. SOLITARY SNIPE *(Gallinago solilaria)* (W)
285. WOOD SINPE *(Gallinago nemoricola)* (W)
286. PINTAIL SNIPE *(Gollinago stenura)* (W/P)
287. SWINHOE'S SNIPE *(Gallinago megala)* (W)
288. GREAT SNIPE *(Gollinago media)* (V)
289. COMMON SNIPE *(Gollinago gallinago)* (W)
290. JACK SNIPE *(Lymnocryptes minimus)* (W/V)

Tringinae: Godwits, curlews, sandpipers, dowitchers, phalaropes & allies

291. BLACK-TAILED GODWIT *(Limosa limosa)* (W/P)
292. WHIMBREL *(Numenius phaeopus)* (W/P)
293. EURASIAN CURLEW *(Numenius arquata)* (W/P)
294. SPOTTED REDSHAWK *(Tringa erythropus)* (W)
295. COMMON REDSHANK *(Tringa totanus)* (W/P)
296. MARSH SANDPIPER *(Tringa stagnatilis)* (W/P)
297. COMMON GREENSHANK *(Tringa nebularia)* (W/P)
298. NORDMANN'S GREENSHANK *(Tringa guttifer)* (?)
299. GREEN SANDPIPER *(Tringa ochropus)* (W)
300. WOOD SANDPIPER *(Tringa glareola)* (W/P)
301. TEREK SANDPIPER *(Xenus cinereus)* (W/P)
302. COMMON SANDPIPER *(Actitis hypoleucos)* (W/P)
303. RUDDY TURNSTONE *(Arenaria interpres)* (W/P)

304. ASIAN DOWITCHER *(Limnodromus semipalmatus)* (?)
305. GREAT KNOT *(Calidris tenuirostris)* (P)
306. RED KNOT *(Calidris canutus)* (P)
307. SANDERLING *(Calidris alba)* (W/P)
308. SPOON-BILLED SANDPIPER *(Calidris pygmeus)* (P/V)
309. LITTLE STINT *(Calidris minuta)* (W/P)
310. RED-NECKED STINT *(Calidris ruficollis)* (W/P)
311. TEMMINCK'S STINT *(Calidris temminckii)* (W/P)
312. LONG-TOED STINT *(Calidris subminuta)* (W)
313. SHARP-TAILED SANDPIPER *(Calidris acuminata)* (V)
314. CURLEW SANDPIPER *(Calidris ferruginea)* (W/P)
315. BROAD-BILLED SANDPIPER *(Limicola falcinellus)* (W/P)
316. RUFF *(Philomachus pugnax)* (W)

ROSTRATULIDAE: Painted-snipes

317. GREATER PAINTED-SNIPE *(Rostratula benghalensis)* (R)

JACANIDAE: Jacanas

318. PHEASANT-TAILED JACANA *(Hydrophasianus chirurgus)* (R)
319. BRONZE-WINGED JACANA *(Metopidius indicus)* (R)

BURHINIDAE: Thick-knees

320. EURASIAN THICK-KNEE *(Burhinus oedicnemus)* (R)
321. GREAT THICK-KNEE *(Esacus recurvirostris)* (R)
322. BEACH THICK-KNEE *(Esacus neglectus)* (R)

CHARADRIIDAE:
Recurvirostrinae: Haematopodini: Oystercatchers

323. EURASIAN OYSTERCATCHER *(Haematopus ostralegus)* (V)

Recurvirostrini: Ibisbill, stilts & avocets

324. IBISBILL *(Ibidorhyncha struthersii)* (W)
325. BLACK-WINGED STILT *(Himantopus himantopus)* (R/?)
326. PIED AVOCET *(Recurviorsrta avosetta)* (w/V)

Charadriinae: Plovers & lapwings

327. PACIFIC GOLDEN PLOVER *(Pluvialis fulva)* (W)
328. GREY PLOVER *(Pluvialis squatarola)* (W/P)
329. COMMON RINGED PLOVER *(Charadrius hiaticula)* (V)
330. LONG-BILLED PLOVER *(Charadrius placidus)* (W)

331. LITTLE RINGED PLOVER *(Charadrius dubius)* (R/W)
332. KENTISH PLOVER *(Charadrius alexandrinus)* (R/W/P)
333. LESSER SAND PLOVER *(Charadrius mongolus)* (W/P)
334. GREATER SAND PLOVER *(Charadrius leschenaultii)* (W/P)
335. NORTHERN LAPWING *(Vanellus vanellus)* (W)
336. YELLOW-WATTLED LAPWING *(Vanellus malabaricus)* (V)
337. RIVER LAPWING *(Vanellus duvaucelii)* (R)
338. GREY-HEADED LAPWING *(Vanellus cinereus)* (W)
339. RED-WATTLED LAPWING *(Vanellus indicus)* (R)

GLAREOLIDAE: Dromadinae: Crab-plover

340. CRAB-PLOVER *(Dromas ardeola)* (?)

Glareolinae: Pratincoles

341. ORIENTAL PRATINCOLE *(Glareola maldivarum)* (B/P/Possibly R)
342. SMALL PRATINCOLE *(Glareola lactea)* (R)

LARIDAE:
Larinae: Stercorariini: Skuas & jaegers

343. POMARINE JAEGER *(Stercorarius pomarinus)* (NB)

Rynchopini: Skimmers

344. INDIAN SKIMMER *(Rynchops albicollis)* (R)

Larini: Gulls

345. MEW GULL *(Larus canus)* (?)
346. HEUGLIN'S GULL *(Larus heuglini)* (?)
347. PALLAS'S GULL *(Larus ichthyaetus)* (W/?)
348. BROWN-HEADED GULL *(Larus brunnicephalus)* (W/P/V)
349. BLACK-HEADED GULL *(Larus ridibundus)* (W)

Sternini: Terns & noddies

350. GULL-BILLED TERN *(Gelochelidon nilotica)* (W)
351. CASPIAN TERN *(Sterna caspia)* (W)
352. RIVER TERN *(Sterna aurantia)* (R)
353. LESSER CRESTED TERN *(Sterna bengalensis)* (NB)
354. GREAT CRESTED TERN *(Sterna bergii)* (R)
355. ROSEATE TERN *(Sterna dougallii)* (NB)
356. BLACK-NAPED TERN *(Sterna sumatrana)* (NB)
357. LITTLE TERN *(sterna albifrons)* (R)
358. BLACK-BELLIED TERN *(sterna acuticauda)* (R)
359. SOOTY TERN *(sterna fuscata)* (V)
360. WHISKERED TERN *(Chlidonias hybridus)* (W/P)

361. WHITE-WINGED TERN *(Chlidonias leucopterus)* (P)
362. BROWN NODDY *(Anous stolidus)* (V)

ACCIPITRIDAE:
Pandioninae: Osprey.

363. OSPERY *(Pandion haliaetus)* (W)

Accipitrinae: Hawks & eagles

364. JERDON'S BAZA *(Aviceda jerdoni)* (R/?)
365. BLACK BAZA *(Aviceda leuphotes)* (R/W/P/?)
366. ORIENTAL HONEY-BUZZARD *(Pernis ptilorhyncus)* (R)
367. BAT HAWK *(Macheiramphus alcinus)* (R)
368. BLACK-SHOULDERED KITE *(Elanus caeruleus)* (R)
369. BLACK-KITE *(Milvus migrans)* (R/W/P)
370. BRAHMINY KITE *(Haliastur indus)* (R)
371. WHITE-BELLIED SEA EAGLE *(Haliaeetus leucogaster)* (R)
372. PALLAS'S FISH EAGLE *(Haliaeetus leucoryphus)* (R/r)
373. WHITE-TAILED EAGLE *(Haliaeetus albicilla)* (?)
374. LESSER FISH EAGLE *(Ichthyophaga humilis)* (R)
375. GREY-HEADED FISH EAGLE *(Ichthyophaga ichthyaetus)* (R)
376. EGYPTIAN VULTURE *(Neophron percnopterus)* (V)
377. WHITE-RUMPED VULTURE *(Gyps bengalensis)* (R/r)
378. LONG-BILLED VULTURE *(Gyps indicus)* (r)
379. HIMALAYAN GRIFFON *(Gyps himalayensis)* (?)
380. CINEREOUS VULTURE *(Aegypius monachus)* (V)
381. RED-HEADED VULTURE *(Sarcogyps calvus)* (r)
382. SHORT-TOED SNAKE EAGLE *(Circaetus gallicus)* (V)
383. CRESTED SERPENT EAGLE *(Spilornis cheela)* (R)
384. WESTERN MARSH HARRIER *(Circus aeruginosus)* (W)
385. EASTERN MARSH HARRIER *(Circus spilonotus)* (W/P)
386. HEN HARRIER *(Circus cyaneus)* (W)
387. PALLID HARRIER *(Circus macrourus)* (W)
388. PIED HARRIER *(Circus melanoleucos)* (W)
389. MONTAGU'S HARRIER *(Circus pygargus)* (V)
390. CRESTED GOSHAWK *(Accipiter trivirgatus)* (R)
391. SHIKRA *(Accipiter badius)* (R)
392. CHINESE SPARROWHAWK *(Accipiter soloensis)* (P)
393. JAPANESE SPARROWHAWK *(Accipiter gularis)* (P)
394. BESRA *(Accipiter virgatus)* (R)
395. EURASIAN SPARROWHAWK *(Accipiter nisus)* (W)

396. NORTHERN GOSHAWK *(Accipiter gentilis)* (W)
397. WHITE-EYED BUZZARD *(Butastur teesa)* (R)
398. RUFOUS-WINGED BUZZARD *(Butastur liventer)* (R)
399. GREY-FACED BUZZARD *(Butastur indicus)* (W/P)
400. COMMON BUZZARD *(Buteo buteo)* (W)
401. LONG-LEGGED BUZZARD *(Buteo rufinus)* (V)
402. BLACK EAGLE *(Ictinaetus malayensis)* (R)
403. LESSER SPOTTED EAGLE *(Aquila pomarina)* (?)
404. GREATER SPOTTED EAGLE *(Aquila clanga)* (W/w)
405. TAWNY EAGLE *(Aquila rapax)* (V)
406. STEPPE EAGLE *(Aquila nipalensis)* (W/V)
407. IMPERIAL EAGLE *(Aquila heliaca)* (V)
408. BONELLI'S EAGLE *(Hieraaetus fasciatus)* (R)
409. BOOTED EAGLE *(Hieraaetus pennatus)* (V)
410. RUFOUS-BELLIED EAGLE *(Hieraaetus kienerii)* (R)
411. CHANGEABLE HAWK EAGLE *(Spizaetus cirrhatus)* (R)
412. MOUNTAIN HAWK EAGLE *(Spizaetus nipalensis)* (R/?)
413. WALLACE'S HAWK EAGLE *(Spizaetus nanus)* (R)

FALCONIDAE: Falcons

414. WHITE-RUMPED FALCON *(Polihierax insignis)* (R)
415. COLLARED FALCONET *(Microhierax caerulescens)* (R)
416. BLACK-THIGHED FALCONET *(Microhierax fringillarius)* (R)
417. LESSER KESTREL *(Falco naumanni)* (w)
418. COMMON KESTREL *(Falco tinnunculus)* (W/P)
419. AMUR FALCON *(Falco amurensis)* (P)
420. EURASIAN HOBBY *(Falco subbuteo)* (W or P)
421. ORIENTAL HOBBY *(Falco severus)* (R)
422. LAGGAR FALCON *(Falco jugger)* (R)
423. PEREGRINE FALCON *(Falco peregrinus)* (R/W/P)

GAVIIDAE: Divers

424. YELLOW-BILLED LOON *(Gavia adamsii)* (?)

PODICIPEDIDAE: Grebes

425. LITTLE GREBE *(Tachybaptus ruficollis)* (R)
426. GREAT CRESTED GREBE *(Podiceps cristatus)* (W)
427. BLACK-NECKED GREBE *(Podiceps nigricollis)* (?)

PHAETHONTIDAE: Tropicbirds

428. RED-BILLED TROPICBIRD *(Phaethon aethereus)* (V)
429. WHITE-TAILED TROPICBIRD *(Phaethon lepturus)* (?)

SULIDAE: Boobies

430. BROWN BOOBY *(Sula leucogaster)* (V)

ANHINGIDAE: Darters

431. DARTER *(Anhinga melanogaster)* (R/r)

PHALACROCORACIDAE: Cormorants

432. LITTLE CORMORANT *(Phalacrocorax niger)* (R/r)
433. INDIAN CORMORANT *(Phalacrocorax fuscicollis)* (R)
434. GREAT CORMORANT *(Phalacrocorax carbo)* (r/w/nb)

ARDEIDAE: Egrets, herons & bitterns

435. LITTLE EGRET *(Egretta garzetta)* (r/W)
436. PACIFIC REEF EGRET *(Egretta sacra)* (R)
437. GREY HERON *(Ardea cinerea)* (r)
438. GOLIATH HERON *(Ardea goliath)* (V)
439. WHITE-BELLIED HERON *(Ardea insignis)* (R/r)
440. GREAT-BILLED HERON *(Ardea sumatrana)* (R)
441. PURPLE HERON *(Ardea purpurea)* (r/W)
442. GREAT EGRET *(Casmerodius albus)* (r/W)
443. INTERMEDIATE EGRET *(Mesophoyx intermedia)* (r/W)
444. CATTLE EGRET *(Bubulcus ibis)* (R/r/W)
445. INDIAN POND HERON *(Ardeola grayii)* (R)
446. CHINESE POND HERON *(Ardeola bacchus)* (W)
447. JAVAN POND HERON *(Ardeola speciosa)* (?)
448. LITTLE HERON *(Butorides striatus)* (R/W)
449. BLACK-CROWNED NIGHT HERON *(Nycticorax nycticorax)* (R/r)
450. MALAYAN NIGHT HERON *(Gorsachius melanolophus)* (?)
451. YELLOW BITTERN *(Ixobrychus sinensis)* (R)
452. VON SCHRENCK'S BITTERN *(Ixobrychus eurhythmus)* (P)
453. CINNAMON BITTERN *(Ixobrychus cinnamomeus)* (R)
454. BLACK BITTERN *(Dupetor flavicollis)* (B)
455. GREAT BITTERN *(Botaurus stellaris)* (W)

THRESKIORNITHIDAE: Ibises & spoonbills

456. GLOSSY IBIS *(Plegadis falcinellus)* (r/W/NB)
457. BLACK-HEADED IBIS *(Threskiornis melanocephalus)* (NB/W)
458. RED-NAPED IBIS *(Pseudibis papillosa)* (R)
459. WHITE-SHOULDERED IBIS *(Pseudibis davisoni)* (r)
460. EURASIAN SPOONBILL *(Platalea leucorodia)* (W)

PELECANIDAE:
Pelecaninae: Pelicans

461. GREAT WHITE PELICAN *(Pelecanus onocrotalus)* (W/V)
462. SPOT-BILLED PELICAN *(Pelecanus philippensis)* (r/nb)

CICONIIDAE:
Ciconiinae: Storks

463. PAINTED STORK *(Mycteria leucocephala)* (r/NB)
464. ASIAN OPENBILL *(Anastomus oscitans)* (NB/P)
465. BLACK STORK *(Ciconia nigra)* (W)
466. WOOLLY-NECKED STORK *(Ciconia episcopus)* (R/r)
467. BLACK-NECKED STORK *(Ephippiorhynchus asiaticus)* (r/?)
468. LESSER ADJUTANT *(Leptoptilos javanicus)* (R/?)
469. GREATER ADJUTANT *(Leptoptilos dubius)* (?)

PROCELLARIIDAE:
Hydrobatinae: Storm-petrels

470. WILSON'S STORM-PETREL *(Oceanites oceanicus)* (V)

PITTIDAE: Pittas

471. EARED PITTA *(Pitta phayrei)* (R)
472. BLUE-NAPED PITTA *(Pitta nipalensis)* (R)
473. RUSTY-NAPED PITTA *(Pitta oatesi)* (R)
474. GIANT PITTA *(Pitta caerulea)* (R)
475. BLUE PITTA *(Pitta cyanea)* (R)
476. GURNEY'S PITTA *(Pitta gurneyi)* (R)
477. HOODED PITTA *(Pitta sordida)* (B)
478. GARNET PITTA *(Pitta granatina)* (R)
479. BLUE-WINGED PITTA *(Pitta moluccensis)* (B)
480. MANGROVE PITTA *(Pitta megarhyncha)* (R)

EURYLAIMIDAE:
Calyptomeninae: Green broadbills

481. GREEN BROADBILL *(Calyptomena viridis)* (R)

Eurylaiminae: Typical broadbills

482. BLACK-AND-RED BROADBILL *(Cymbirhynchus macrorhynchos)* (R)
483. LONG-TAILED BROADBILL *(Psarisomus dalhousiae)* (R)
484. SILVER-BREASTED BROADBILL *(Serilophus lunatus)* (R)
485. BANDED BROADEBILL *(Eurylaimus javanicus)* (R)

486. BLACK-AND-YELLOW BROADBILL
(*Eurylaimus ochromalus*) (R)
487. DUSKY BROADBILL (*Corydon sumatranus*) (R)

IRENIDAE: Fairy bluebirds & leafbirds

488. ASIAN FAIRY BLUEBIRD (*Irena puella*) (R)
489. GREATER GREEN LEAFBIRD (*Chloropsis sonnerati*) (R)
490. LESSER GREEN LEAFBIRD (*Chloropsis cyanopogon*) (R)
491. BLUE-WINGED LEAFBIRD (*Chloropsis cochinchinensis*) (R)
492. GOLDEN-FRONTED LEAFBIRD (*Chloropsis aurifrons*) (R)
493. ORANGE BELLIED LEAFBIRD (*Chloropsis hardwickii*) (R)

LANIIDAE: Shrikes

494. TIGER SHRIKE (*Lanius tigrinus*) (P)
495. BROWN SHRIKE (*Lanius cristatus*) (W/P)
496. BURMESE SHRIKE (*Lanius collurioides*) (R/W)
497. LONG-TAILED SHRIKE (*Lanius schach*) (R/?)
498. GREY-BACKED SHRIKE (*Lanius tephronotus*) (W)

CORVIDAE:
Pachycephalinae: Pachycephalini: Whistlers & allies

499. MANGROVE WHISTLER (*Pachycephala grisola*) (R)

Corvinae: Corvini: Jays, magpies, treepies, nutcrackers, crows & allies

500. CRESTED JAY (*Platylophus galericulatus*) (R)
501. BLACK MAGPIE (*Platysmurus leucopterus*) (R)
502. EURASIAN JAY (*Garrulus glandarius*) (R)
503. YELLOW-BILLED BLUE MAGPIE (*Urocissa flavirostris*) (R)
504. RED-BILLED BLUE MAGPIE (*Urocissa erythrorhyncha*) (R)
505. COMMON GREEN MAGPIE (*Cissa chinensis*) (R)
506. RUFOUS TREEPIE (*Dendrocitta vagabunda*) (R)
507. GREY TREEPIE (*Dendrocitta formosae*) (R)
508. COLLARED TREEPIE (*Dendrocitta frontalis*) (R)
509. RACKET-TAILED TREEPIE (*Crypsirina temia*) (R)
510. HOODED TREEPIE (*Crypsirina cucullata*) (R)
511. RATCHET-TAILED TREEPIE (*Temnurus temnurus*) (R)
512. BLACK-BILLED MAGPIE (*Pica pica*) (R)
513. SPOTTED NUTCRACKER (*Nucifraga caryocatactes*) (R)
514. HOUSE CROW (*Corvus splendens*) (R)
515. LARGE-BILLED CROW (*Corvus macrorhynchos*) (R)

516. COLLARED CROW (*Corvus torquatus*) (?)

Artamini: Woodswallows & allies

517. ASHY WOODSWALLOW (*Artamus fuscus*) (R)
518. WHITE-BREASTED WOODSWALLOW (*Artamus leucorynchus*) (R)

Oriolini: Orioles, cuckooshrikes, trillers, minivets & flycatcher-shrikes

519. DARK-THROATED ORIOLE (*Oriolus xanthonotus*) (R)
520. BLACK-NAPED ORIOLE (*Oriolus chinensis*) (R/W)
521. SLENDER-BILLED ORIOLE (*Oriolus tenuirostris*) (R)
522. BLACK-HOODED ORIOLE (*Oriolus xanthornus*) (R)
523. MAROON ORIOLE (*Oriolus traillii*) (R)
524. LARGE CUCKOOSHRIKE (*Coracina macei*) (R)
525. INDOCHINESE CUCKOOSHRIKE (*Coracina polioptera*) (R)
526. BLACK-WINGED CUCKOOSHRIKE (*Coracina melaschistos*)(R/W)
527. LESSER CUCKOOSHRIKE (*Coracina fimbriata*) (R)
528. BLACK-HEADED CUCKOOSHRIKE (*Coracina melanoptera*) (W)
529. PIED TRILLER (*Lalage nigra*) (?)
530. ROSY MINIVET (*Pericrocotus roseus*) (R)
531. SWINHOE'S MINIVET (*Pericrocotus cantonensis*) (W)
532. ASHY MINIVET (*Pericrocotus divaricatus*) (W)
533. SMALL MINIVET (*Pericrocotus cinnamomeus*) (R)
534. FIERY MINIVET (*Pericrocotus igneus*) (R)
535. WHITE-BELLIED MINIVET (*Pericrocotus erythropygius*) (R)
536. GREY-CHINNED MINIVET (*Pericrocotus solaris*) (R)
537. LONG-TAILED MINIVET (*Pericrocotus ethologus*) (R/W)
538. SHORT-BILLED MINIVET (*Pericrocotus brevirostris*) (R)
539. SCARLET MINIVET (*Pericrocotus flammeus*) (R/W)
540. BAR-WINGED FLYCATCHER-SHRIKE (*Hemipus picatus*) (R)
541. BLACK-WINGED FLYCATCHER-SHRIKE (*Hemipus hirundinaceus*) (R)

Dicrurinae: Rhipidurini: Fantails

542. YELLOW-BELLIED FANTAIL (*Rhipidura hypoxantha*) (R)
543. WHITE-THROATED FANTAIL (*Rhipidura albicollis*) (R)

544. WHITE-BROWED FANTAIL *(Rhipidura aureola)* (R)
545. PIED FANTAIL *(Rhipidura javanica)* (R)

Dicrurini: Drongos

546. BLACK DRONGO *(Dicrurus macrocercus)* (R/W)
547. ASHY DRONGO *(Dicrurus leucophaeus)* (R/W)
548. CROW-BILLED DRONGO *(Dicrurus annectans)* (W/P/?)
549. BRONZED DRONGO *(Dicrurus aeneus)* (R)
550. LESSER RACKET-TAILED DRONGO *(Dicrurus remifer)* (R)
551. SPANGLED DRONGO *(Dicrurus hottentottus)* (R/?)
552. ANDAMAN DRONGO *(Dicrurus andamanensis)* (R)
553. GREATER RACKET-TAILED DRONGO *(Dicrurus paradiseus)* (R)

Monarchini: Monarchs, paradise-flycatchers & allies

554. BLACK-NAPED MONARCH *(Hypothymis azurea)* (R/W)
555. ASIAN PARADISE - FLYCATCHER *(Terpsiphone paradisi)* (R/W/B/P)

Aegithininae: Ioras

556. COMMON IORA *(Aegithina tiphia)* (R)
557. GREEN IORA *(Aegithina viridissima)* (R)
558. GREAT IORA *(Aegithina lafresnayei)* (R)

Malaconotinae: Vangini: Philentomas, woodshrikes & allies

559. RUFOUS- WINGED PHILENTOMA *(Philentoma pyrhopterum)* (R)
560. MAROON-BREASTED PHILENTOMA *(Philentoma velatum)* (R)
561. LARGE WOODSHRIKE *(Tephrodornis gularis)* (R)
562. COMMON WOODSHRIKE *(Tephrodornis pondicerianus)* (R)

CINCLIDAE: Dippers

563. WHITE-THROATED DIPPER *(Cinclus cinclus)* (W)
564. BROWN DIPPER *(Cinclus pallasii)* (R)

MUSCICAPIDAE:
Turdinae: Thrushes & shortwings

565. BLUE-CAPPED ROCK THRUSH *(Monticola cinclorhynchus)* (?)
566. WHITE-THROATED ROCK THRUSH *(Monticola gularis)* (W)

567. CHESTNUT-BELLIED ROCK THRUSH *(Monticola rufiventris)* (R)
568. BLUE ROCK THRUSH *(Monticola solitarius)* (Possibly R/W/P)
569. BLUE WHISTLING THRUSH *(Myophonus caeruleus)* (R/W)
570. ORANGE-HEADED THRUSH *(Zoothera citrina)* (R/B/?/P)
571. SIBERIAN THRUSH *(Zoothera sibirica)* (P)
572. PLAIN-BACKED THRUSH *(Zoothera mollissima)* (Probably R)
573. LONG-TAILED THRUSH *(Zoothera dixoni)* (R/W/?)
574. SCALY THRUSH *(Zoothera dauma)* (R/W)
575. LONG-BILLED THRUSH *(Zoothera monticola)* (R)
576. DARK-SIDED THRUSH *(Zoothera marginata)* (R)
577. BLACK-BREASTED THRUSH *(Turdus dissimilis)* (R)
578. WHITE-COLLARED BLACKBIED *(Turdus albocinctus)* (?)
579. GREY-WINGED BLACKBIRD *(Turdus boulboul)* (W/?)
580. EURASIAN BLACKBIRD *(Turdus merula)* (?)
581. CHESTNUT THRUSH *(Turdus rubrocanus)* (W)
582. GREY-SIDED THRUSH *(Turdus feae)* (W)
583. EYEBROWED THRUSH *(Turdus obscurus)* (W)
584. DARK-THROATED THRUSH *(Turdus ruficollis)* (W)
585. DUSKY THRUSH *(Turdus naumanni)* (W)
586. RUSTY-BELLIED SHORTWING *(Brachypteryx hyperythra)* (?)
587. GOULD'S SHORTWING *(Brachypteryx stellata)* (R)
588. LESSER SHORIWING *(Brachypteryx leucophrys)* (R)
589. WHITE-BROWED SHORTWING *(Brachypteryx montana)* (R)

Muscicapinae: Muscicapini: Old World flycatchers

590. FULVOUS-CHESTED JUNGLE FLYCATCHER *(Rhinomyias olivacea)* (R)
591. DARK-SIDED FLYCATCHER *(Muscicapa sibirica)* (R/Probably B/W/?)
592. ASIAN BROWN FLYCATCHER *(Muscicapa dauurica)* (R/W)
593. BROWN-STREAKED FLYCATCHER *(Muscicapa williamsoni)* (R)
594. BROWN-BREASTED FLYCATCHER *(Muscicapa muttui)* (P/?)
595. FERRUGINOUS FLYCATCHER *(Muscicapa ferruginea)* (P/?)
596. SLATY-BACKED FLYCATCHER *(Ficedula hodgsonii)* (R/W)
597. RUFOUS- GORGETED FLYCATCHER *(Ficedula strophiata)* (R/W)
598. RED-THROATED FLYCATCHER *(Ficedula parva)* (W)

599. WHITE-GORGETED FLYCATCHER *(Ficedula monileger)* (R)
600. RUFOUS-BROWED FLYCATCHER *(Ficedula solitaris)* (R)
601. SNOWY-BROWED FLYCATCHER *(Ficedula hyperythra)* (R)
602. LITTLE PIED FLYCATCHER *(Ficedula westermanni)* (R)
603. ULTRAMARINE FLYCATCHER *(Ficedula superciliaris)* (R)
604. SLATY-BLUE FLYCATCHER *(Ficedula tricolor)* (R)
605. SAPPHIRE FLYCATCHER *(Ficedula sapphira)* (? Probably R)
606. BULE-AND-WHITE FLYCATCHER *(Cyanoptila cyanomelana)* (P)
607. VERDITER FLYCATCHER *(Eumyias thalassina)* (R/?)
608. LARGE NILTAVA *(Niltava grandis)* (R)
609. SMALL NILTAVA *(Niltava macgrigoriae)* (R)
610. RUFOUS-BELLIED NILTAVA *(Niltava sundara)* (R/W)
611. VIVID NILTAVA *(Niltava vivida)* (?)
612. WHITE-TAILED FLYCATCHER *(Cyornis concretus)* (R)
613. HAINAN BLUE FLYCATCHER *(Cyornis hainanus)* (R)
614. PALE-CHINNED FLYCATCHER *(Cyornis poliogenys)* (R)
615. PALE BLUE FLYCATCHER *(Cyornis unicolor)* (R)
616. BLUE-THROATED FLYCATCHER *(Cyornis rubeculoides)* (R/W/P)
617. HILL BLUE FLYCATCHER *(Cyornis banyumas)* (R/W/?)
618. TICKELL'S BLUE FLYCATCHER *(Cyornis tickelliae)* (R)
619. PYGMY BLUE FLYCATCHER *(Muscicapella hodgsoni)* (R/?)
620. GREY-HEADED CANARY FLYCATCHER *(Culicicapa ceylonensis)* (R/W)

Saxicolini: Chats & allies

621. SIBERIAN RUBYTHROAT *(Luscinia calliope)* (W)
622. WHITE-TAILED RUBYTHROAT *(Luscinia pectoralis)* (R)
623. BLUETHROAT *(Luscinia svecica)* (W)
624. FIRETHROAT *(Luscinia pectardens)* (?)
625. INDIAN BLUE ROBIN *(Luscinia brunnea)* (R)
626. SIBERIAN BLUE ROBIN *(Luscinia cyane)* (W)
627. ORANGE-FLANKED BUSH ROBIN *(Tarsiger cyanurus)* (Probably B/W)
628. GOLDEN BUSH ROBIN *(Tarsiger chrysaeus)* (R/W)
629. WHITE-BROWED BUSH ROBIN *(Tarsiger indicus)* (R)
630. RUFOUS-BREASTED BUSH ROBIN *(Tarsiger hyperythrus)* (Probably B)

631. ORIENTAL MAGPIE ROBIN *(Copsychus saularis)* (R)
632. WHITE-RUMPED SHAMA *(Copsychus malabaricus)* (R)
633. BLACK REDSTART *(Phoenicurus ochruros)* (W)
634. HODGSON'S REDSTART *(Phoenicurus hodgsoni)* (W)
635. WHITE-THROATED REDSTART *(Phoenicurus schisticeps)* (?)
636. DAURIAN REDSTART *(Phoenicurus auroreus)* (W/may be R)
637. BLUE-FRONTED REDSTART *(Phoenicurus frontalis)* (W/?/Probably B)
638. WHITE-CAPPED WATER REDSTART *(Chaimarrornis leucocephalus)* (R/?)
639. PLUMBEOUS WATER REDSTART *(Rhyacornis fuliginosus)* (R/?)
640. WHITE-BELLIED REDSTART *(Hodgsonius phaenicuroides)* (R/W)
641. WHITE-TAILED ROBIN *(Myiomela leucura)* (R)
642. GRANDALA *(Grandala coelicolor)* (?)
643. LITTLE FORKTAIL *(Enicurus scouleri)* (R)
644. CHESTNUT-NAPED FORKTAIL *(Enicurus ruficapillus)* (R)
645. BLACK-BACKED FORKTAIL *(Enicurus immaculatus)* (R)
646. SLATY-BACKED FORKTAIL *(Enicurus schistaceus)* (R)
647. WHITE-CROWNED FORKTAIL *(Enicurus leschenaulti)* (R)
648. SPOTTED FORKTAIL *(Enicurus maculatus)* (R)
649. PURPLE COCHOA *(Cochoa purpurea)* (R)
650. GREEN COCHOA *(Cochoa viridis)* (R)
651. COMMON STONECHAT *(Saxicola torquata)* (R/W)
652. WHITE-TAILED STONECHAT *(Saxicola leucura)* (R)
653. PIED BUSHCHAT *(Saxicola caprata)* (R)
654. JERDON'S BUSHCHAT *(Saxicola jerdoni)* (R)
655. GREY BUSHCHAT *(Saxicola ferrea)* (R/W)
656. ISABELLINE WHEATEAR *(Oenanthe isabellina)* (V)

STURNIDAE:
Sturnini: Starlings & mynas

657. ASIAN GLOSSY STARLING *(Aplonis panayensis)* (R)
658. SPOT-WINGED STARLING *(Saroglossa spiloptera)* (W)
659. CHESTNUT-TAILED STARLING *(Sturnus malabaricus)* (R)
660. PURPLE-BACKED STARLING *(Sturnus sturninus)* (P)
661. WHITE-SHOULDERED STARLING *(Sturnus sinensis)* (W)
662. COMMON STARLING *(Sturnus vulgaris)* (V)
663. WHITE-CHEEKED STARLING *(Sturnus cineraceus)* (V)

664. ASIAN PIED STARLING *(Sturnus contra)* (R)
665. BLACK-COLLARED STARLING *(Sturnus nigricollis)* (R)
666. VINOUS-BREASTED STARLING *(Sturnus burmannicus)* (R)
667. COMMON MYNA *(Acridotheres tristis)* (R)
668. JUNGLE MYNA *(Acridotheres fuscus)* (R)
669. WHITE-VENTED MYNA *(Acridotheres grandis)* (R)
670. COLLARED MYNA *(Acridotheres albocinctus)* (R)
671. CRESTED MYNA *(Acridotheres cristatellus)* (?)
672. GOLDEN-CRESTED MYNA *(Ampeliceps coronatus)* (R)
673. HILL MYNA *(Gracula religiosa)* (R)

SITTIDAE:
Sittinae: Nuthatches

674. CHESTNUT-VENTED NUTHATCH *(Sitta nagaensis)* (R)
675. CHESTNUT-BELLIED NUTHATCH *(Sitta castanea)* (R)
676. WHITE-TAILED NUTHATCH *(Sitta himalayensis)* (R)
677. WHITE-BROWED NUTHATCH *(Sitta victoriae)* (R)
678. VELVET-FRONTED NUTHATCH *(Sitta frontalis)* (R)
679. GIANT NUTHATCH *(Sitta magna)* (R)
680. BEAUTIFUL NUTHATCH *(Sitta formosa)* (R)

CERTHIIDAE:
Certhiinae: Certhiini: Treecreepers

681. EURASIAN TREECREEPER *(Certhia familiaris)* (R)
682. BAR-TAILED TREECREEPER *(Certhia himalayana)* (R)
683. RUSTY-FLANKED TREECREEPER *(Certhia nipalensis)* (R)
684. BROWN-THROATED TREECREEPER *(Certhia discolor)* (R)

Troglodytinae: Wrens

685. WINTER WREN *(Troglodytes troglodytes)* (R)

PARIDAE: Remizinae: Penduline tits

686. FIRE-CAPPED TIT *(Cephalopyrus flammiceps)* (W)

Parinae: Typical tits

687. BLACK-BIBBED TIT *(Parus hypermelaena)* (R)
688. RUFOUS-VENTED TIT *(Parus rubidiventris)* (R)
689. COAL TIT *(Parus ater)* (R)
690. GREY-CRESTED TIT *(Parus dichrous)* (R)
691. GREAT TIT *(Parus major)* (R)
692. GREEN-BACKED TIT *(Parus monticolus)* (R)

693. YELLOW- CHEEKED TIT *(Parus spilonotus)* (R)
694. YELLOW-BROWED TIT *(Sylviparus modestus)* (R)
695. SULTAN TIT *(Melanochlora sultanea)* (R)

AEGITHALIDAE: Long-tailed tits

696. BLACK-THROATED TIT *(Aegithalos concinnus)* (R)
697. BLACK-BROWED TIT *(Aegithalos bonvaloti)* (R)

HIRUNDINIDAE:
Hirundininae: Martins and swallows

698. SAND MARTIN *(Riparia riparia)* (W)
699. PLAIN MARTIN *(Riparia paludicola)* (R)
700. DUSKY CRAG MARTIN *(Hirundo concolor)* (R)
701. BARN SWALLOW *(Hirundo rustica)* (W/P)
702. PACIFIC SWALLOW *(Hirundo tahitica)* (R)
703. WIRE-TAILED SWALLOW *(Hirundo smithii)* (R)
704. RED-RUMPED SWALLOW *(Hirundo daurica)* (W)
705. STRIATED SWALLOW *(Hirundo striolata)* (R)
706. NORTHERN HOUSE MARTIN *(Delichon urbica)* (W)
707. ASIAN HOUSE MARTIN *(Delichon dasypus)* (W)
708. NEPAL HOUSE MARTIN *(Delichon nipalensis)* (R)

REGULIDAE: Crests & allies

709. COMMON GOLDCREST *(Regulus regulus)* (?)

PYCNONOTIDAE: Bulbuls

710. CRESTED FINCHBILL *(Spizixos canifrons)* (R)
711. STRAW-HEADED BULBUL *(Pycnonotus zeylanicus)* (R)
712. STRIATED BULBUL *(Pycnonotus striatus)* (R)
713. BLACK-HEADED BULBUL *(Pycnonotus atriceps)* (R)
714. BLACK-CRESTED BULBUL *(Pycnonotus melanicterus)* (R)
715. SCALY-BREASTED BULBUL *(Pycnonotus squamatus)* (R)
716. GREY-BELLIED BULBUL *(Pycnonotus cyaniventris)* (R)
717. RED-WHISKERED BULBUL *(Pycnonotus jocosus)* (R)
718. BROWN-BREASTED BULBUL *(Pycnonotus xanthorrhous)* (R)
719. RED-VENTED BULBUL *(Pycnonotus cafer)* (R)
720. SOOTY-HEADED BULBUL *(Pycnonotus aurigaster)* (R)
721. PUFF-BACKED BULBUL *(Pycnonotus eutilotus)* (R)
722. STRIPE-THROATED BULBUL *(Pycnonotus finlaysoni)* (R)

723. FLAVESCENT BULBUL *(Pycnonotus flavescens)* (R)
724. YELLOW-VENTED BULBUL *(Pycnonotus goiavier)* (R)
725. OLIVE-WINGED BULBUL *(Pycnonotus plumosus)* (R)
726. STREAK-EARED BULBUL *(Pycnonotus blanfordi)* (R)
727. RED-EYED BULBUL *(Pycnonotus brunneus)* (R)
728. SPECTACLED BULBUL *(Pycnonotus erythropthalmos)* (R)
729. WHITE-THROATED BULBUL *(Alophoixus flaveolus)* (R)
730. PUFF-THROATED BULBUL *(Alophoixus pallidus)* (R)
731. OCHRACEOUS BULBUL *(Alophoixus ochraceus)* (R)
732. GREY-CHEEKED BULBUL *(Alophoixus bres)* (R)
733. YELLOW-BELLIED BULBUL *(Alophoixus phaeocephalus)* (R)
734. HAIRY-BACKED BULBUL *(Tricholestes criniger)* (R)
735. OLIVE BULBUL *(Iole virescens)* (R)
736. GREY-EYED BULBUL *(Iole propinqua)* (R)
737. BUFF-VENTED BULBUL *(Iole olivacea)* (R)
738. STREAKED BULBUL *(Ixos malaccensis)* (R)
739. ASHY BULBUL *(Hemixos flavala)* (R)
740. MOUNTAIN BULBUL *(Hypsipetes mcclellandii)* (R)
741. BLACK BULBUL *(Hypsipetes leucocephalus)* (R/W)
742. WHITE-HEADED BULBUL *(Hypsipetes thompsoni)* (R)

CISTICOLIDAE: African warblers (cisticolas, prinias & allies)

743. ZITTING CISTICOLA *(Cisticola juncidis)* (R)
744. BRIGHT-HEADED CISTICOLA *(Cisticola exilis)* (R)
745. STRIATED PRINIA *(Prinia criniger)* (R)
746. BROWN PRINIA *(Prinia polychroa)* (R)
747. HILL PRINIA *(Prinia atrogularis)* (R)
748. RUFESCENT PRINIA *(Prinia rufescens)* (R)
749. GREY-BREASTED PRINIA *(Prinia hodgsonii)* (R)
750. YELLOW-BELLIED PRINIA *(Prinia flaviventris)* (R)
751. PLAIN PRINIA *(Prinia inornata)* (R)

ZOSTEROPIDAE: White-eyes

752. CHESTNUT- FLANKED WHITE-EYE *(Zosterops erythropleurus)* (W)
753. ORIENTAL WHITE-EYE *(Zosterops palpebrosus)* (R)
754. JAPANESE WHITE-EYE *(Zosterops japonicus)* (W)

SYLVIIDAE:
Acrocephalinae: Tesias, warblers, tailorbirds & allies

755. CHESTNUT-HEADED TESIA *(Tesia castaneocoronata)* (R)
756. SLATY-BELLIED TESIA *(Tesia olivea)* (R)
757. GREY-BELLIED TESIA *(Tesia cyaniventer)* (R)
758. ASIAN STUBTAIL *(Urosphena squameiceps)* (W)
759. PALE-FOOTED BUSH WARBLER *(Cettia pallidipes)* (R)
760. BROWNISH-FLANKED BUSH WARBLER *(Cettia fortipes)* (R)
761. ABERRANT BUSH WARBLER *(Cettia flavolivacea)* (R)
762. YELLOWISH-BELLIED BUSH WARBLER *(Cettia acanthizoides)* (?)
763. GREY-SIDED BUSH WARBLER *(Cettia brunnifrons)* (R)
764. SPOTTED BUSH WARBLER *(Bradypterus thoracicus)* (R/W)
765. CHINESE BUSH WARBLER *(Bradypterus tacsanowskius)* (W)
766. BROWN BUSH WARBLER *(Bradypterus luteoventris)* (R/W)
767. RUSSET BUSH WARBLER *(Bradypterus mandelli)* (R)
768. LANCEOLATED WARBLER *(Locustella lanceolata)* (W)
769. RUSTY-RUMPED WARBLER *(Locustella certhiola)* (W)
770. BLACK-BROWED REED WARBLER *(Acrocephalus bistrigiceps)* (W)
771. PADDYFIELD WARBLER *(Acrocephalus agricola)* (W/V)
772. MANCHURIAN REED WARBLER *(Acrocephalus tangorum)* (W)
773. BLUNT-WINGED WARBLER *(Acrocephalus concinens)* (W)
774. BLYTH'S REED WARBLER *(Acrocephalus dumetorum)* (W)
775. ORIENTAL REED WARBLER *(Acrocephalus orientalis)* (W/P)
776. CLAMOROUS REED WARBLER *(Acrocephalus stentoreus)* (R)
777. THICK-BILLIED WARBLER *(Acrocephalus aedon)* (W)
778. MOUNTAIN TAILORBIRD *(Orthotomus cuculatus)* (R)
779. COMMON TAILORBIRD *(Orthotomus sutorius)* (R)
780. DARK-NECKED TAILORBIRD *(Orthotomus atrogularis)* (R)
781. RUFOUS-TAILED TAILORBIRD *(Orthotomus sericeus)* (R)
782. ASHY TAILORBIRD *(Orthotomus ruficeps)* (R)
783. DUSKY WARBLER *(Phylloscopus fuscatus)* (W)
784. TICKELL'S LEAF WARBLER *(Phylloscopus affinis)* (W)

785. BUFF-THROATED WARBLER *(Phylloscopus subaffinis)* (W)
786. YELLOW-STREAKED WARBLER *(Phylloscopus armandii)* (R/W)
787. RADDE'S WARBLER *(Phylloscopus schwarzi)* (W)
788. BUFF-BARRED WARBLER *(Phylloscopus pulcher)* (R/W/?)
789. ASHY-THROATED WARBLER *(Phylloscopus maculipennis)* (R)
790. LEMON-RUMPED WARBLER *(Phylloscopus chloronotus)* (W/?)
791. CHINESE LEAF WARBLER *(Phylloscopus sichuanensis)* (W)
792. YELLOW-BROWED WARBLER *(Phylloscopus inornatus)* (W)
793. HUME'S WARBLER *(Phylloscopus humei)* (W)
794. ARCTIC WARBLER *(Phylloscopus borealis)* (W)
795. GREENISH WARBLER *(Phylloscopus trochiloides)* (W)
796. TWO-BARRED WARBLER *(Phylloscopus plumbeitarsus)* (W)
797. PALE-LEGGED LEAF WARBLER *(Phylloscopus tenellipes)* (W)
798. LARGE-BILLED LEAF WARBLER *(Phylloscopus magnirostris)* (R or B/W)
799. EASTERN CROWNED WARBLER *(Phylloscopus coronatus)* (W/P)
800. EMEI LEAF WARBLER *(Phylloscopus emeiensis)* (?)
801. BLYTH'S LEAF WARBLER *(Phylloscopus reguloides)* (R/W)
802. WHITE-TAILED LEAF WARBLER *(Phylloscopus davisoni)* (R)
803. YELLOW-VENTED WARBLER *(Phylloscopus cantator)* (W)
804. GREY-CROWNED WARBLER *(Seicercus tephrocephalus)* (R/W)
805. PLAIN-TAILED WARBLER *(Seicercus soror)* (W)
806. WHISTLER'S WARBLER *(Seicercus whistleri)* (R)
807. GREY-HOODED WARBLER *(Seicercus xanthoschistos)* (R)
808. WHITE-SPECTACLED WARBLER *(Seicercus affinis)* (R)
809. GREY-CHEEKED WARBLER *(Seicercus poliogenys)* (R)
810. CHESTNUT-CROWNED WARBLER *(Seicercus castaniceps)* (R)
811. BROAD-BILLED WARBLER *(Tickellia hodgsoni)* (R)
812. RUFOUS-FACED WARBLER *(Abroscopus albogularis)* (R)
813. BLACK-FACED WARBLER *(Abroscopus schisticeps)* (R)
814. YELLOW-BELLIED WARBLER *(Abroscopus superciliaris)* (R)

Megalurinae: Grassbirds

815. STRIATED GRASSBIRD *(Megalurus palustris)* (R)

816. RUFOUS-RUMPED GRASSBIRD *(Graminicola bengalensis)* (r)

Garrulacinae: Laughingthrushes

817. WHITE-CRESTED LAUGHINGTHRUSH *(Garrulax leucolophus)* (R)
818. LESSER NECKLACED LAUGHINGTHRUSH *(Garrulax monileger)* (R)
819. GREATER NECKLACED LAUGHING-THRUSH *(Garrulax pectoralis)* (R)
820. STRIATED LAUGHINGTHRUSH *(Garrulax striatus)* (R)
821. WHITE-NECKED LAUGHINGTHRUSH *(Garrulax strepitans)* (R)
822. RUFOUS-NECKED LAUGHINGTHRUSH *(Garrulax ruficollis)* (R)
823. CHESINUT-BACKED LAUGHINGTHRUSH *(Garrulax nuchalis)* (R)
824. BLACK-THROATED LAUGHINGTHRUSH *(Garrulax chinensis)* (R)
825. YELLOW-THROATED LAUGHINGTHRUSH *(Garrulax galbanus)* (R)
826. RUFOUS-VENTED LAUGHINGTRUSH *(Garrulax gularis)* (R)
827. MOUSTACHED LAUGHINGTHRUSH *(Garrulax cineraceus)* (R)
828. RUFOUS-CHINNED LAUGHINGTHRUSH *(Garrulax rufogularis)* (R)
829. SPOTTED LAUGHINGTHRUSH *(Garrulax ocellatus)* (R)
830. GREY-SIDED LAUGHINGTHRUSH *(Garrulax caerulatus)* (R)
831. SPOT-BREASTED LAUGHINGTHRUSH *(Garrulax merulinus)* (R)
832. WHITE-BROWED LAUGHINGTHRUSH *(Garrulax sannio)* (R)
833. STRIPED LAUGHINGTHRUSH *(Garrulax virgatus)* (R)
834. BROWN-CAPPED LAUGHINGTHRUSH *(Garrulax austeni)* (R)
835. BLUE-WINGED LAUGHINGTRUSH *(Garrulax squamatus)* (R)
836. SCALY LAUGHINGTHRUSH *(Garrulax subunicolor)* (R)
837. BLACK-FACED LAUGHINGTHRUSH *(Garrulax affinis)* (R)
838. CHESTNUT-CROWNED LAUGHINGTHRUSH *(Garrulax erythrocephalus)* (R)
839. RED-TAILED LAUGHINGTHRUSH *(Garrulax milnei)* (R)
840. RED-FACED LIOCICHLA *(Liocichla phoenicea)* (R)

Sylvinae: Timaliini: Babblers

841. WHITE-CHESTED BABBLER *(Trichastoma rostratum)* (R)

842. FERRUGINOUS BABBLER *(Trichastoma bicolor)* (R)
843. ABBOTT'S BABBLER *(Malacocincla abbotti)* (R)
844. SHORT-TAILED BABBLER *(Malacocincla malaccensis)* (R)
845. BUFF-BREASTED BABBLER *(Pellorneum tickelli)* (R)
846. SPOT-THROATED BABBLER *(Pellorneum albiventre)* (R)
847. PUFF-THROATED BABBLER *(Pellorneum ruficeps)* (R)
848. BLACK-CAPPED BABBLER *(Pellorneum capistratum)* (R)
849. MOUSTACHED BABBLER *(Malacopteron magnirostre)* (R)
850. RUFOUS-CROWNED BABBLER *(Malacopteron magnum)*(R)
851. LARGE SCIMITAR BABBLER *(Pomatorhinus hypoleucos)* (R)
852. SPOT-BREASTED SCIMITAR BABBLER *(Pomatorhinus erythrocnemis)* (R)
853. RUSTY-CHEEKED SCIMITAR BABBLER *(Pomatorhinus erythrogenys)* (R)
854. WHITE-BROWED SCIMITAR BABBLER *(Pomatorhinus schisticeps)* (R)
855. STREAK-BREASTED SCIMITAR BABBLER*(Pomatorhinus ruficollis)* (R)
856. RED-BILLED SCIMITAR BABBLER *(Pomatorhinus ochraceiceps)* (R)
857. CORAL-BILLED SCIMITAR BABBLER *(Pomatorhinus ferruginosus)* (R)
858. SLENDER-BILLED SCIMITAR BABBLER *(Xiphirhynchus superciliaris)* (R)
859. LONG-BILLED WREN BABBLER *(Rimator malacoptilus)* (R)
860. LIMESTONE WREN BABBLER *(Napothera crispifrons)* (R)
861. STREAKED WREN BABBLER *(Napothera brevicaudata)* (R)
862. EYEBROWED WREN BABBLER *(Napothera epilepidota)* (R)
863. SCALY-BREASTED WREN BABBLER *(Pnoepyga albiventer)* (R)
864. PYGMY WREN BABBLER *(Pnoepyga pusilla)* (R)
865. BAR-WINGED WREN BABBLER *(Spelaeornis troglodytoides)* (R)
866. SPOTTED WREN BABBLER *(Spelaeornis formosus)* (R)
867. LONG-TAILED WREN BABBLER *(Spelaeornis chocolatinus)* (R)
868. WEDGE-BILLED WREN BABBLER *(Sphenocichla humei)* (R)
869. RUFOUS-FRONTED BABBLER *(Stachyris rufifrons)* (R)
870. RUFOUS-CAPPED BABBLER *(Stachyris ruficeps)* (R)
871. GOLDEN BABBLER *(Stachyris chrysaea)* (R)
872. GREY-THROATED BABBLER *(Stachyris nigriceps)* (R)

873. SNOWY-THROATED BABBLER *(Stachyris oglei)* (R)
874. SPOT-NECKED BABBLER *(Stachyris striolata)* (R)
875. CHESTNUT-WINGED BABBLER *(Stachyris erythroptera)* (R)
876. STRIPED TIT BABBLER *(Macronous gularis)* (R)
877. CHESTNUT-CAPPED BABBLER *(Timalia pileata)* (R)
878. YELLOW-EYED BABBLER *(Chrysomma sinense)* (R)
879. JERDON'S BABBLER *(Chrysomma altirostre)* (R)
880. STRIATED BABBLER *(Turdoides earlei)* (R)
881. WHITE-THROATED BABBLER *(Turdoides gularis)* (R)
882. SLENDER-BILLED BABBLER *(Turdoides longirostris)* (R)
883. CHINESE BABAX *(Babax lanceolatus)* (R)
884. SILVER-EARED MESIA *(Leiothrix argentauris)* (R)
885. RED-BILLED LEIOTHRIX *(Leiothrix lutea)* (R)
886. CUTIA *(Cutia nipalensis)* (R)
887. BLACK-HEADED SHRIKE BABBLER *(Pteruthius rufiventer)* (R)
888. WHITE-BROWED SHRIKE BABBLER *(Pteruthius flaviscapis)* (R)
889. GREEN SHRIKE BABBLER *(Pteruthius xanthochlorus)* (R)
890. BLACK-EARED SHRIKE BABBLER *(Pteruthius melanotis)* (R)
891. CHESTNUT-FRONTED SHRIKE BABBLER *(Pteruthius aenobarbus)* (R)
892. WHITE-HOODED BABBLER *(Gampsorhynchus rufulus)* (R)
893. RUSTY-FRONTED BARWING *(Actinodura egertoni)* (R)
894. SPECTACLED BARWING *(Actinodura ramsayi)* (R)
895. STREAK-THROATED BARWING *(Actinodura waldeni)* (R)
896. BLUE-WINGED MINLA *(Minla cyanouroptera)* (R)
897. CHESTNUT-TAILED MINLA *(Minla strigula)* (R)
898. RED-TAILED MINLA *(Minla ignotincta)* (R)
899. GOLDEN-BREASTED FULVETTA *(Alcippe chrysotis)* (R)
900. YELLOW-THROATED FULVETTA *(Alcippe cinerea)* (R)
901. RUFOUS-WINGED FULVETTA *(Alcippe castaneceps)* (R)
902. WHITE-BROWED FULVETTA *(Alcippe vinipectus)* (R)
903. STREAK-THROATED FULVETTA *(Alcippe cinereiceps)* (R)
904. RUFOUS-THROATED FULVETTA *(Alcippe rufogularis)* (R)
905. RUSTY-CAPPED FULVETTA *(Alcippe dubia)* (R)
906. BROWN-HEADED FULVETTA *(Alcippe ludlowi)* (?)

907. BROWN-CHEEKED FULVETTA *(Alcippe poioicephala)* (R)
908. GREY-CHEEKED FULVETTA *(Alcippe morrisonia)* (R)
909. NEPAL FULVETTA *(Alcippe nipalensis)* (R)
910. RUFOUS-BACKED SIBIA *(Heterophasia annectens)* (R)
911. GREY SIBIA *(Heterophasia gracilis)* (R)
912. DARK-BACKED SIBIA *(Heterophasia melanoleuca)* (R)
913. BLACK-HEADED SIBIA *(Heterophasia desgodinsi)* (R)
914. BEAUTIFUL SIBIA *(Heterophasia pulchella)* (R)
915. LONG-TAILED SIBIA *(Heterophasia picaoides)* (R)
916. STRIATED YUHINA *(Yuhina castaniceps)* (R)
917. WHITE-NAPED YUHINA *(Yuhina bakeri)* (R)
918. WHISKERED YUHINA *(Yuhina flavicollis)* (R)
919. BURMESE YUHINA *(Yuhina humilis)* (R)
920. STRIPE-THROATED YUHINA *(Yuhina gularis)* (R)
921. WHITE-COLLARED YUHINA *(Yuhina diademata)* (R)
922. RUFOUS-VENTED YUHINA *(Yuhina occipitalis)* (R)
923. BLACK-CHINNED YUHINA *(Yuhina nigrimenta)* (R)
924. WHITE-BELLIED YUHINA *(Yuhina zantholeuca)* (R)
925. FIRE-TAILED MYZORNIS *(Myzornis pyrrhoura)* (R)
926. GREAT PARROTBILL *(Conostoma oemodium)* (R)
927. BROWN PARROTBILL *(Paradoxornis unicolor)* (R)
928. GREY-HEADED PARROTBILL *(Paradoxornis gularis)* (R)
929. SPOT-BERASTED PARROTBILL *(Paradoxornis guttaticollis)* (R)
930. BROWN-WINGED PARRORBILL *(Paradoxornis brunneus)* (R)
931. FULVOUS PARROTBILL *(Paradoxornis fulvifrons)* (R)
932. BLACK-THROATED PARROTBILL *(Paradoxornis nipalensis)* (R)
933. GOLDEN PARROTBILL *(Paradoxornis verreauxi)* (R)
934. SHORT-TAILED PARROTBILL *(Paradoxornis davidianus)* (R)
935. LESSER RUFOUS-HEADED PARROTBILL *(Paradoxornis atrosuperciliaris)* (R)
936. GREATER RUFOUS-HEADED PARROTBILL *(Paradoxornis ruficeps)* (R)

ALAUDIDAE: Larks

937. AUSTRALASIAN BUSHLARK *(Mirafra javanica)* (R)
938. BENGAL BUSHLARK *(Mirafra assamica)* (R)
939. BURMESE BUSHLARK *(Mirafra microptera)* (R)
940. INDOCHINESE BUSHLARK *(Mirafra marionae)* (R)
941. GREATER SHORT-TOED LARK *(Calandrella brachydactyla)* (W/V)
942. ASIAN SHORT-TOED LARK *(Calandrella cheleensis)* (V)
943. SAND LARK *(Calandrella raytal)* (R)
944. ORIENTAL SKYLARK *(Alauda gulgula)* (R/W)

NECTARINIIDAE:
Nectariniinae: Dicaeini: Flowerpeckers

945. YELLOW-BREASTED FLOWERPECKER *(Prionochilus maculatus)* (R)
946. CRIMSON-BREASTED FLOWERPECKER *(Prionochilus percussus)* (R)
947. THICK-BILLED FLOWERPECKER *(Dicaeum agile)* (R)
948. YELLOW-VENTED FLOWERPECKER *(Dicaeum chrysorrheum)* (R)
949. YELLOW-BELLIED FLOWERPECKER *(Dicaeum melanoxanthum)* (R)
950. ORANGE-BELLIED FLOWERPECKER *(Dicaeum trigonostigma)* (R)
951. PALE-BILLED FLOWERPECKER *(Dicaeum erythrorynchos)* (R)
952. PLAIN FLOWERPECKER *(Dicaeum concolor)* (R)
953. FIRE-BREASTED FLOWERPECKER *(Dicaeum ignipectus)* (R)
954. SCARLET-BACKED FLOWERPECKER *(Dicaeum cruentatum)* (R)

Nectariniini: Sunbirds & spiderhunters

955. PLAIN SUNBIRD *(Anthreptes simplex)* (R)
956. BROWN-THROATED SUNBIRD *(Anthreptes malacensis)* (R)
957. RED-THROATED SUNBIRD *(Anthreptes rhodolaema)* (R)
958. RUBY-CHEEKED SUNBIRD *(Anthreptes singalensis)* (R)
959. PURPLE-NAPED SUNBIRD *(Hypogramma hypogrammicum)* (R)
960. PURPLE-RUMPED SUNBIRD *(Nectarinia zeylonica)* (R)
961. PURPLE-THROATED SUNBIRD *(Nectarinia sperata)* (R)
962. COPPER-THROATED SUNBIRD *(Nectarinia calcostetha)* (R)
963. OLIVE-BACKED SUNBIRD *(Nectarinia jugularis)* (R)
964. PURPLE SUNBIRD *(Nectarinia asiatica)* (R)
965. MRS GOULD'S SUNBIRD *(Aethopyga gouldiae)* (R)
966. GREEN-TAILED SUNBIRD *(Aethopyga nipalensis)* (R)
967. BLACK-THROATED SUNBIRD *(Aethopyga saturata)* (R)

968. CRIMSON SUNBIRD *(Aethopyga siparaja)* (R)
969. FIRE-TAILED SUNBIRD *(Aethopyga ignicauda)* (R/V)
970. LITTLE SPIDERHUNTER *(Arachnothera longirostra)* (R)
971. YELLOW-EARED SPIDERHUNTER *(Arachnothera chrysogenys)* (R)
972. GREY-BREASTED SPIDERHUNTER *(Arachnothera affinis)* (R)
973. STREAKED SPIDERHUNTER *(Arachnothera magna)* (R)

PASSERIDAE:
Passerinae: Sparrows

974. HOUSE SPARROW *(Passer domesticus)* (R)
975. RUSSET SPARROW *(Passer rutilans)* (R)
976. PLAIN-BACKED SPARROW *(Passer flaveolus)* (R)
977. EURASIAN TREE SPARROW *(Passer montanus)* (R)

Motacillinae: Wagtails & pipits

978. FOREST WAGTAIL *(Dendronanthus indicus)* (W/P)
979. WHITE WAGTAIL *(Motacilla alba)* (R/B/W/P)
980. CITRINE WAGTAIL *(Motacilla citreola)* (W)
981. YELLOW WAGTAIL *(Motacilla flava)* (W/P)
982. GREY WAGTAIL *(Motacilla cinerea)* (W/P)
983. WHITE-BROWED WAGTAIL *(Motacilla maderaspatensis)* (?)
984. RICHARD'S PIPIT *(Anthus richardi)* (W/P)
985. PADDYFIELD PIPIT *(Anthus rufulus)* (R)
986. BLYTH'S PIPIT *(Anthus godlewskii)* (W)
987. LONG-BILLED PIPIT *(Anthus similis)* (R)
988. TREE PIPIT *(Anthus trivialis)* (V)
989. OLIVE-BACKED PIPIT *(Anthus hodgsoni)* (R/B/P/W)
990. RED-THROATED PIPIT *(Anthus cervinus)* (W)
991. ROSY PIPIT *(Anthus roseatus)* (W/Probably B)
992. BUFF-BELLIED PIPIT *(Anthus rubescens)* (V)

Prunellinae: Accentors

993. ALPINE ACCENTOR *(Prunella collaris)* (?)
994. RUFOUS-BREASTED ACCENTOR *(Prunella strophiata)* (?)
995. MAROON-BACKED ACCENTOR *(Prunella immaculata)* (?)

Ploceinae: Weavers

996. BLACK-BREASTED WEAVER *(Ploceus benghalensis)* (?)
997. STREAKED WEAVER *(Ploceus manyar)* (R)
998. BAYA WEAVER *(Ploceus phillippinus)* (R)
999. ASIAN GOLDEN WEAVER *(Ploceus hypoxanthus)* (R)

Estrildinae: Estrildini: Estrildine finches (Red Avadavat, parrotfinches, munias & Java Sparrow)

1000. RED AVADAVAT *(Amandava amandava)* (R)
1001. PIN-TAILED PARROTFINCH *(Erythrura prasina)* (R)
1002. WHITE-RUMPED MUNIA *(Lanchura striata)* (R)
1003. SCALY-BREASTED MUNIA *(Lonchura punctulata)* (R)
1004. WHITE-BELLIED MUNIA *(Lanchura leucogastra)* (R)
1005. BLACK-HEADED MUNIA *(Lanchura malacca)* (R)
1006. JAVA SPARROW *(Padda oryzivora)* (?)

FRINGILLIDAE:
Fringillinae: Carduelini: Finches, siskins, crossbills, grosbeaks & allies

1007. YELLOW-BREASTED GREENFINCH *(Carduelis spinoides)* (R)
1008. BLACK-HEADED GREENFINCH *(Carduelis ambigua)* (R)
1009. TIBETAN SISKIN *(Carduelis thibetana)* (?)
1010. PLAIN MOUNTAIN FINCH *(Leucosticte nemoricola)* (?)
1011. DARK-BREASTED ROSEFINCH *(Carpodacus nipalensis)* (? Probably R/W)
1012. COMMON ROSEFINCH *(Carpodacus erythrinus)* (W)
1013. VINACEOUS ROSEFINCH *(Carpodacus vinaceus)* (R)
1014. DARK-RUMPED ROSEFINCH *(Carpodacus edwardsii)* (R)
1015. SPOT-WINGED POSEFINCH *(Carpodacus rodopeplus)* (R)
1016. CRIMSON-BROWED FINCH *(Propyrrhula subhimachala)* (R)
1017. SCARLET FINCH *(Haematospiza sipahi)* (R)
1018. RED CROSSBILL *(Loxia curvirostra)* (R)
1019. BROWN BULLFINCH *(Pyrrhula nipalensis)* (R)
1020. GREY-HEADED BULLFINCH *(Pyrrhula erythaca)* (R)
1021. YELLOW-BILLED GROSBEAK *(Eophona migratoria)* (V)
1022. COLLARED GROSBEAK *(Mycerobas affinis)* (R)
1023. SPOT-WINGED GROSBEAK *(Mycerobas melanozanthos)* (R)
1024. WHITE-WINGED GROSBEAK *(Mycerobas carnipes)* (R)
1025. GOLD-NAPED FINCH *(Pyrrhoplectes epauletta)* (R)

Emberizinae: Emberizini: Buntings & allies

1026. CRESTED BUNTING *(Melophus lathami)* (R)
1027. GODLEWSKI'S BUNTING *(Emberiza godlewskii)* (?)

1028. TRISTRAM'S BUNTING *(Emberiza tristrami)*
(W)
1029. CHESTNUT-EARED BUNTING *(Emberiza fucata)* (W)
1030. LITTLE BUNTING *(Emberiza pusilla)* (W)
1031. YELLOW-THROATED BUNTING *(Emberiza elegans)* (?)
1032. YELLOW-BREASTED BUNTING *(Emberiza aureola)* (W)
1033. CHESTNUT BUNTING *(Emberiza rutila)* (W)
1034. BLACK-FACED BUNTING *(Emberiza spodocephala)* (W)
1035. PALLAS'S BUNTING *(Emberiza pallasi)* (V)

Ref:

A *Field Guide to the Birds of Thailand and South-East Asia* by Craig Robson (2000)
Forktail, No.17, August 2001 "Birds recorded during two expeditions to north Myanmar (Burma)" King *et al*
Oriental Bird Club, Bulletin 33, June 2001 "From the field" compiled by Craig Robson
Oriental Bird Club, Bulletin 34, December 2001 "From the field" compiled by Craig Robson
Crab Plover – one record at Let Kok Kon (KMMT)
****
Report on distribution of birds in Hkakaborazi region by Zin Oo (1997)
- Expedition to Hkakaborazi National Park, Myanmar, 31 January–16 March 2001 by John H. Rappole (2001)
- UKNL (pers. com.)

List of Birds Protected by Law in Myanmar

In exercise of the powers conferred upon him by the Protection of Wildlife and Wild Plants and Conservation of Natural Areas Law of 1994, the Director-General of the Forest Department issued the Decree No 583/94 dated October 26, 1994, proclaiming certain species of mammals, birds and reptiles to be "protected animals" in three categories, namely Totally Protected Animals, Protected Animals and Seasonally Protected Animals. The bird species listed in the Decree are shown below:

A. Totally Protected Animals

1. Peafowls, Pheasants — Family *Phasianidae*
2. Masked finfoot — *Heliopais personata*
3. White-winged Woodduck — *Cairina scutulata*
4. Greater Adjutant Stork — *Leptotilos dubius*
5. Lesser Adjutant Stork — *Leptotilos javanicus*
6. Comb Duck — *Sarkidiornis melanotos*
7. Bar-headed Goose — *Anser indicus*
8. Mandarin Duck — *Aix galericulata*
9. Pink-headed Duck — *Rhodonessa caryophyllacea*
10. Ferruginous Duck — *Aythya nyroca*
11. Baer's Pochard — *Aythya baeri*
12. Nordmann's Greenshank — *Tringa guttifer*
13. Wood Snipe — *Gallinago nemoricola*
14. White-bellied Heron — *Ardea insignis*
15. Oriental Darter — *Anhinga melanogaster*
16. Spot-billed Pelican — *Pelecanus philippensis*
17. Eastern White Pelican — *Pelecanus onocrotalus*
18. White-shoulder Ibis — *Pseudibis davisoni*
19. Indian Skimmer — *Rynchops albicollis*
20. Sarus Crane — *Grus antigone*
21. Common Crane — *Grus grus*
22. Demoiselle Crane — *Anthropoides virgo*
23. Hornbills — Family *Bucerotidae*
24. Eagle, Kite, Falcon, Hawk, Vulture (Birds of Prey) — Family *Accipitridae*
25. Gurney's Pitta — *Pitta gurneyi*
26. White-throated Babbler — *Turdoides gularis*
27. Hooded Treepie — *Crypsirina cuculata*
28. Myanma Yuhina — *Yuhina humilis*
29. White-browed Nuthatch — *Sitta victoriae*
30. Rails, Crakes — Family *Rallidae*
31. Water Cock — *Gallicrex cinerea*
32. Great Cormorant — *Phalacrocorax carbo*
33. Bitterns — Family *Ardeidae*
34. Hoopoe — *Upupa epoc*
35. Trogons — Family *Trogonidae*
36. Woodpeckers — Family *Picidae*
37. Great Bustard — *Otis tarda*
38. Owls, Fish Owls, Barn Owl — Family *Strigiformes*
39. Osprey — *Pandion haliaetus*
40. Falcon — Family *Falconidae*
41. Nicobar Pigeon — *Caloenas nicobarica*
42. Indian Shag — *Phalacrocorax fuscicollis*
43. Brown Gannet — *Sulaleucogaster plotus*
44. Grackle — *Gracula religiosa*
45. Storks — Family *Ciconiidae*
46. Ibises, Spoonbills — Family *Threskiornithidae*
47. Geese, Ducks — Family *Anatidae*
48. Jacanas — Family *Jacanidae*
49. Plover, Avocet, Pratincole, Lapwing, Curlew, Shank, Sandpiper, Snipe — *Shorebirds species*
50. Gulls, Terns — Family *Laridae*

B. Protected Animals

1. Magpie — Family *Corvidae*
2. Treepie — Family *Corvidae*
3. Jay — Family *Corvidae*
4. Tit — Family *Paridae*
5. Laughing Thrush — *Garrulax species*
6. Yuhina — *Yuhina species*
7. Nuthatch — Family *Sittidae*
8. Sibia — *Heterophasia species*
9. Fairy Bluebird — *Irena puella*
10. European Wren — *Troglodytes troglodytes*
11. Dipper — *Cinclus species*
12. Tree creeper — Family *Certhidae*
13. Accentors — *Prunella species*
14. Oriole — *Oriolus species*
15. Glossy Starling — *Aplonis panayensis*
16. European Starling — *Sturnus species*
17. Baya Weaverbird — *Ploceus philippinus*
18. Finch — Family *Fringillidae*/Subfamily *Carduelinae*
19. Skylark — Family *Alaudidae*
20. White eye — Family *Zosteropidae*
21. Broad bill — Family *Eurylaimidae*
22. Barbet — Family *Capitonidae*
23. Malcoha — *Phoenicophaeus species*
24. Red-bearded Bee-eater — *Nyctyornis amictus*
25. Yellow-backed Honey guide — *Indicator xanthonotus fulvus*

26. Parakeet/Parrot	Family *Psittacidae*
27. Kingfisher	*Alcedinidae species*
28. Edible-nest Swiftlet	*Collocalia fuciphaga*
29. Black-nest Swiftlet	*Collocalia maxima*
30. Purple Heron	*Ardea purpurea*
31. Grey Heron	*Ardea cinerea*
32. Heron	*Ardea species*
33. Great Egret	*Egretta alba*
34. Reef Egret	*Egretta sacra*
35. Chinese Pond Heron	*Ardeola bacchus*
36. Javan Pond Heron	*Ardeola speciosa continentalis*
37. Little Green Heron	*Butorides species*
38. Frogmouth	Family *Podargidae*
39. Sunbird	Family *Nectarinidae*
40. Flowerpecker	Family *Dicaeidae*
41. Pittas	Family *Pittidae*
42. Green Pigeon	Family *Columbidae*
43. Minivets	Family *Campephagidae*

C. Seasonally Protected Animals
(From March 15 to September 30)

1. Partridge/Francolin	Family *Phasianidae* Subfamily *Perdicinae*
2. Quails	*Turnix species*
3. Iora	*Aegithina tiphia*
4. Leafbirds	*Chloropsis species*
5. Doves	Family *Columbidae*
6. Common Moorhen	*Gallinula chloropus*
7. Purple Swamphen	*Porphyrio porphyrio*
8. Bulbul	Family *Pycnonotidae*
9. Robins, Redstarts, Chats, Forktails	Family *Turdidae*
10. Paradise Flycatcher	Family *Muscicapidae*
11.Cuckoo/Koel	Family *Cuculidae* Subfamily *Cuculinae*
12. Nightjars	Family *Caprimulgidae*
13. Drongos	Family *Dicruridae*

(Nomenclature and arrangements are as given in the Decree)

Glossary

Aquatic	Living in or frequenting water, eg. ducks, grebes
Arboreal	Living in trees
Bizat	*Eupatorium odoratum*, a kind of weed that colonises open spaces
Casque	An enlargement on upper surface of the bill like a helmet eg. in hornbills
Cere	Soft, swollen area at base of upper mandible eg. in parrots, hawks
Crepuscular	Of twilight
Deciduous	Tree or forest shedding leaves annually
Dimorphic	Occuring in two forms
Diurnal	Active in day-time
Endemic	Restricted to a locality (Myanmar has 4 endemic bird species)
Evergreen	Tree or forest having green leaves all the year round
Ferruginous	Rust-coloured, reddish brown
Gregarious	Living in flocks
Gular	Of the throat
Indaing	Dry dipterocarp forest without bamboos
Insectivorous	Insect-eating
Kaing	*Saccharum* spp, tall, thick elephant grass
Letpan	*Bombax malabaricum*, Silk-Cotton Tree
Malar	Of the cheek
Monogamous	Having only one mate at a time
Nocturnal	Active in the night
Nuchal	Of the nape of the neck
Ochraceous	Dark brownish yellow
Ocular	Of the eye
Omnivorous	Feeding on both plant and animal food
Orbital	Border round eye of bird
Pectoral	Of the breast
Polygamous	Having more than one mate at one time
Polymorphic	Occuring in many forms
Raptor	Bird of prey
Second growth	New growth of trees, bushes etc following deforestation
Speculum	Lustrous coloured patch on wings of birds eg. in ducks
Taungya	Shifting cultivation in the forest
Terrestrial	Living on ground
Thetke	*Imperata cylindrica*, grass used for thatching
Vinaceous (Vinous)	Red wine coloured

Myanmar
Existing Protected Areas
As of December, 2002

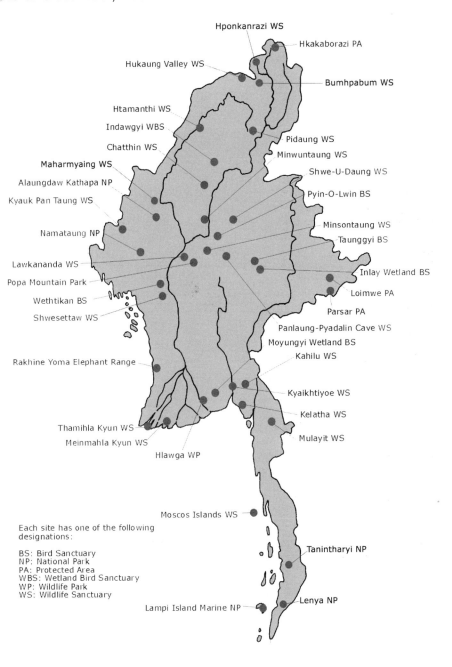

Hponkanrazi WS

Hkakaborazi PA

Hukaung Valley WS

Bumhpabum WS

Htamanthi WS

Indawgyi WBS

Chatthin WS

Pidaung WS

Minwuntaung WS

Maharmyaing WS

Shwe-U-Daung WS

Alaungdaw Kathapa NP

Kyauk Pan Taung WS

Pyin-O-Lwin BS

Namataung NP

Minsontaung WS

Taunggyi BS

Lawkananda WS

Inlay Wetland BS

Popa Mountain Park

Loimwe PA

Wethtikan BS

Parsar PA

Shwesettaw WS

Panlaung-Pyadalin Cave WS

Moyungyi Wetland BS

Kahilu WS

Rakhine Yoma Elephant Range

Kyaikhtiyoe WS

Kelatha WS

Thamihla Kyun WS

Meinmahla Kyun WS

Mulayit WS

Hlawga WP

Moscos Islands WS

Each site has one of the following
designations:

BS: Bird Sanctuary
NP: National Park
PA: Protected Area
WBS: Wetland Bird Sanctuary
WP: Wildlife Park
WS: Wildlife Sanctuary

Tanintharyi NP

Lenya NP

Lampi Island Marine NP

Source: Forest Department

List of Protected Areas Established in Myanmar
(up to the end of 2002)

Sr. No.	Name	Year est.	Total area sq.miles	Location	Key species protected
1.	Pidaung Wildlife Sanctuary	1918	269.46	Kachin State	Elephant, Gaur, Banteng, Sambar, Tiger, Leopard, Bear
2.	Shwe-U-Daung Wildlife Sanctuary	1918/1929	125.85	Mandalay Div./ Shan State	Rhinoceros, Elephant, Gaur, Banteng, Sambar, Serow, Tiger, Bear
3.	Pyin-O-Lwin Bird Sanctuary	1918	49.13	Mandalay Div.	Barking deer, Pheasant
4.	Moscos Islands Wildlife Sanctuary	1927	18.99	Taninthayi Div.	Barking deer. Sambar, Swiftlet
5.	Kahilu Wildlife Sanctuary	1928	61.99	Karen State	Rhinoceros, Serow, Mouse deer, Hog deer
6.	Taunggyi Bird Sanctuary	1930	6.2	Shan State	Avifauna
7.	Mulayit Wildlife Sanctuary	1936	53.49	Karen State	Barking deer, Tiger, Leopard
8.	Wethtikan Bird Sanctuary	1939	1.70	Magwe Div.	Wetland birds
9.	Shwesettaw Wildlife Sanctuary	1940	213.4	Magwe Div.	Eld's deer, Sambar, Barking deer, Gaur
10.	Chatthin Wildlife Sanctuary	1941	104.0	Sagaing Div.	Eld's deer, Sambar, Barking deer,"
11.	Kelatha Wildlife Sanctuary	1942	9.45	Mon State	Serow, Avifauna"
12.	Thamihla Kyun Wildlife Sanctuary	1970	0.34	Ayeyarwady Div.	Marine Turtle
13.	Htamanthi Wildlife Sanctuary	1971	830.4	Sagaing Div.	Rhinoceros, Elephant, Gaur, Tiger
14.	Minwuntaung Wildlife Sanctuary	1972	79.49	Sagaing Div.	Barking deer, Avifauna
15.	Hlawga Wildlife Park	1982	2.41	Yangon Div.	Enclosed wildlife park. Sambar, Barking deer, Hog deer, Eld' deer, Mythun, Migratory birds
16.	Inlay Wetland Bird Sanctuary	1985	248	Shan State	Wetland and migratory birds
17.	Moyungyi Wetland Bird Sanctuary	1988	40	Bago Div.	Migratory birds
18.	Alaungdaw Kathapa National Park	1989	616.843	Sagaing Div.	Elephant, Tiger, Leopard, Gaur, Sambar, Serow, Bear
19.	Popa Mountain Park	1989	49.63	Mandalay Div.	Barking deer, Leopard, Geomorphologic features
20.	Meinmahla Kyun Wildlife Sanctuary	1993	52.78	Ayeyarwady Div.	Mangrove crocodiles, Birds
21.	Lampi Island Marine National Park	1996	79.09	Tanintharyi Div.	Coral reefs, Mouse, deer and Salon ethnic culture
22.	Hkakaborazi National Park	1996	1472	Kachin State	Takin, Musk deer, Red goral, Black barking deer
23.	Loimwe Protected Area	1996	16.54	Shan State	Tiger, Bear, Pangolin, Pheasant

24.	Parsar Protected Area	1996	29.74	Shan State	Jungle fowl, Chinese pangolin
25.	Namataung National Park	1997	279	Chin State	Gaur, Serow, Goral and Avifauna
26.	Lawkananda Wildlife Sanctuary	1997	0.18	Mandalay Div.	Avifauna, Cultural diversity
27.	Indawgyi Wetland Bird Sanctuary	1999	299.32	Kachin State	Elephant, Tiger, Sambar, Leopard, Bear, Serow, Gaur
28.	Kyaikhtiyoe Wildlife Sanctuary	2001	60.32	Mon State	Tiger, Goral, Gaur, Sambar, Monkey
29.	Minsontaung Wildlife Sanctuary	2001	8.725	Mandalay Div.	Barking deer, Rabbit, Dhole, Reptiles, Land tortoises, Wild Cat, Snakes
30.	Hukaung Valley Wildlife Sanctuary	2001	2494	Kachin State	Elephant, Leopard, Tiger, Gaur, Sambar, Bear, Wildboar, Serow
31.	Kyauk Pan Taung Wildlife Sanctuary	2001	51.2	Chin State	Serow, Goral, Sambar, Leopard, Clouded Leopard, Wild Cats, Barking deer, Wildboar
32.	Hponkanrazi Wildlife Sanctuary	2001	1044	Kachin State	Barking deer, Avifauna, Red Goral, Gibbon, Wild dogs, Mangooses
33.	Rakhine Yoma Elephant Range	2002	677.88	Rakhine State	Elephant, Gaur, Leopard, Jackal, Bear
34.	Panlaung-Pyadalin Cave Wildlife Sanctuary	2002	128.88	Shan State	Elephant, Tiger, Leopard, Gaur, Banteng, Golden Cat, Clouded Leopard, Serow, Gibbon
35.	Maharmyaing Wildlife Sanctuary	2002	455.75	Sagaing Div.	Sambar, Wildboar, Banteng, Feline, Gibbon, Wild dogs, Mangooses
36.	Lenya National Park	2002	682	Tanintharyi Div.	Tapir, Elephant, Monkeys, Barking deer, Sambar, Wildboar, Bear, Mouse deer, Wild cats, Pangolin, Lizards, Birds, Tiger
37.	Tanintharyi National Park	2002	1000	Tanintharyi Div.	Sambar, Barking deer, Serow, Goral, Leopard, Wild elephant, Birds, Tiger
38.	Bumhpabum Wildlife Sanctuary	2002	719	Kachin State	Elephant, Gaur, Serow, Deer spp:, Clouded Leopard, Golden Cat, Jackal, Goral, Mancaques, Civets, Bear, Leopard, Pheasant, Hornbills

References

Ali, Salim. 1943. *The Book of Indian Birds*. The Bombay Natural History Society.

Baker, E. C. Stuart. 1922–1928. *The Fauna of British India including Ceylon and Burma, Birds* Vol.I to VIII. Taylor and Francis, London.

Beebe, William. 1937. *Pheasants, Their Lives and Homes*. Robert Hale Limited, London.

Bhushan, Bharat, *et al*, 1993. *A Field Guide to the Waterbirds of Asia*. Wild Bird Society of Japan.

Boonsong Lekagul, Edward W. Cronin Jr. 1974. *Bird Guide of Thailand*, 2nd Ed. Association for the Conservation of Wildlife, Bangkok.

Boonsong Lekagul, Philip D. Round. 1991. *A Guide to the Birds of Thailand*. Saha Karn Bhaet Co., Ltd.

Brown, Leslie, Dean Amadon.1968. E*agles, Hawks and Falcons of the World*, 2 Vols. Country Life Books.

Delacour, Jean. 1954–1959. *The Waterfowl of the World*. Vol. I to III. Country Life Limited, London.

Eve, Roland, Anne-Marie Guigue, 2000. *Birds of Thailand*. Times Media Private Ltd.

Forshaw, Joseph M., William T. Cooper. 1973. *Parrots of the World*. Lansdowne Press.

Grimmett, Richard, Carol Inskipp, Tim Inskipp. 1999. *Birds of India, Pakistan, Nepal, Bangladesh, Bhutan, Sri Lanka and the Maldives*. Princeton University Press.

Grzimek, Bernhard (Ed). 1973. *Grzimek's Animal Life Encyclopedia* Vol 7, 8 and 9 Birds. Van Nostrand Reinhold Company.

Hvass, Hans. 1963. *Birds of the World*. Methuen & Co Ltd.

King, B. F, Edward C. Dickinson, Martin W. Woodcock. 1978. *A Field Guide to the Birds of South-East Asia*. Collins.

Lay, U Maung Maung, 1950. *Hnget-tha-bin* (Birds of Burma), Burma Translation Society, Yangon.

Makatsch, Wolfgang. 1966. *Wir Bestimmen Die Vögel Europas*. Neumann Verlag.

Myanmar Language Commission. 1993. *Myanmar-English Dictionary*, Department of the Myanmar Language Commision, Ministry of Education.

Perrins, Christopher, Ad Cameron, 1976. *Bird Life – An Introduction to the World of Birds*. Elsevier Phaidon.

Peterson, Roger, Guy Mountfort, P. A. D. Hollom, 1961. *A Field Guide to the Birds of Britain and Europe*. Collins.

Robson, Craig. 2000. *A Field Guide to the Birds of Thailand and South-East Asia*. Asia Books Co., Ltd.

Scott, Peter. 1957. *A Coloured Key to the Wildfowl of the World*. The Wildfowl Trust, England.

Smythies, Bertram E. 1968. *The Birds of Borneo*, 2nd Ed, Oliver & Boyd.

Smythies, Bertram E. 1953. *The Birds of Burma*, 2nd Ed, Oliver & Boyd.

Smythies, Bertram E. 1986. *The Birds of Burma*, 3rd Ed, Nimrod Press Ltd and Silvio Mattacchione & Co.

Wildash, Philip. 1968. *Birds of South Vietnam*. Charles E. Tuttle Co Publishers.

Index

Birds of Myanmar

Birds of Myanmar

Index by Myanmar Names

အက္ခရာဝလီ

(ယှဉ်တွဲဖော်ပြပါ နံပါတ်များမှာ ငှက်များ၏ အမှတ်စဉ်နံပါတ်များဖြစ်ပါသည်)

စာပြောက်	၃၄၅		တုံးစပ်	၁၃၅
စာဖြူ	၂၀၄		တုံးမြီးကွက်	၁၃၄
စာဘုန်းကြီး	၃၄၂		ထုတ္တရူ	၄၁
စာမဲ	၂၀၆		ထန်းစေ့မှုတ်	၁၅၀
စာဝတီး	၃၄၀ ၃၄၄ ၃၄၅ ၃၄၆		ထပ်တလျူ	၄၁
စာဝါ	၃၄၃ ၃၄၂		ဒီးဒုတ်	၂၂
စက္ကဝါက်	၁၃		ဒေါင်း	၁၀
စင်ရော်	၁၂၆		ဒေါင်းကုလား	၉
စင်ရော်ခေါင်းမဲ	၁၂၅		ဒေါင်းမင်း	၉
စစ်စလီ	၁၁ ၁၂		ဒေါင်းလန်းခြေထောက်	၁၁၈
စစ်စလီခေါင်းမဲ	၁၂		ဒိန်ညင်း	၄၄
စစ်တလိုင်း	၁၂၀		ဒုံးမြီးကွက်	၁၃၄
စွေ့	၃၀၃		နဖားကြီး	၁၉၂
စွန်	၁၃၄		နဖားကြူး	၁၉၄
စွန်ခေါင်းဖြူ	၁၃၅		နို့စုတ်	၂၂၂
ဆနွင်းဝါ	၁၉၈ ၁၉၉		နို့ပြီစုတ်	၂၂၆ ၂၂၇ ၂၂၈ ၂၂၉
ဆက်ရက်	၂၄၂		ပတုံငှက်	၅၀
ဆက်ရက်ကျား	၂၃၉		ပဿူးစာ	၃၄၄
ဆက်ရက်ခေါင်းဖြူ	၂၄၀		ပုစဉ်ထိုး	၅၁
ဆက်ရက်တောင်ပံဖြူ	၂၃၈		ပုစဉ်ထိုးမြီးပြာ	၅၂
ဆက်ရက်လည်နက်	၂၄၀		ပုစဉ်ထိုးရင်ဝါ	၃၂
ဆင်ပိန်ညင်း	၄၅		ပဲခူးစာ	၃၄၄
ဆတ်ဖျိုင်း	၁၆၃		ပင်လယ်ပုံလွှား	၆၈
ဇရက်	၂၄၂		ပေါင်တုတ်	၁၀၀
ဇီဝဇိုး	၆၈		ပန်းရည်စုပ်	၂၂၆ ၂၂၇ ၂၂၈
ဇီးကွက်	၈၁		ပန်းရည်စုပ်ကျောဝါ	၂၂၉
တီတီတွတ်	၁၂၀		ပိန်ညင်း	၄၄ ၄၆ ၄၇ ၄၈ ၄၉
တီးတုတ်	၂၂		ပိန်ညင်းကျား	၄၉
တဲသလိပ်ဆွယ်	၂၃၁		ပိန်ညင်းခေါင်းမဲ	၄၇
တောကျီးကန်း	၁၉၆		ပိန်ညင်းရင်ဖြူ	၄၆
တောကြက်	၅		ဖျားတူငှက်	၅၀
တောဆက်ရက်	၂၄၃		ပုံလွှား	၃၀ ၃၂ ၃၃ ၃၆ ၃၃
တောဘဲ	၁၄		ပုံလွှားကြီး	၃၀
တောလုံ့ငှက်	၃၅		ဖိုးခေါင်	၃၂
တောသားသဲပိတ်လွှယ်	၂၃၁		ဖောင်တုတ်	၁၀၀
တင်ကျိုး	၁၅၂ ၁၅၃ ၁၅၄		ဖျိုင်း	၁၅၅
တောင်ငုံး	၁၅၆ ၁၅၇ ၁၅၈ ၁၅၉		ဖျိုင်းငန်	၁၅၈
တောင်ခေါင်းငှက်	၈၃		ဖျိုင်းနှမ်း	၁၆၀
တောင်ပိစ္ဆူး	၃၉		ဖျိုင်းအောက်	၁၆၀
တောင်ဘီစူး	၃၉		ဖြူ	၂၆၃
တစ်တီတူး	၁၂၀		ဗွတ်	၂၃၈ ၃၁၆ ၂၆၂ ၂၆၄
တိန်ညင်း	၄၄ ၄၆ ၄၇ ၄၈ ၄၉			၂၆၅ ၂၆၆ ၂၆၇
တုံးကုလား	၁၃၃		ဗွတ်ကလုံ	၂၆၀

About the Authors

U Kyaw Nyunt Lwin

A veterinary surgeon by profession, and he started studying birds when he first joined Yangon Zoological Gardens in 1974. His dual role as the Director of Yangon Zoological Gardens until 1998 and as the Project Director of the UNDP-funded Nature Conservation and National Parks Project from 1980 to 1985, had transformed him into a *"zoo-cum-wildlife man"*, and led him to write articles and books on wildlife. His works, *Mammals of Myanmar* and *Wild Cats* were published by Sarpay Beikhman, the official government publishing house in 1984.

He was also a member of the drafting committee of the Protection of Wildlife and Wild Plants and Conservation of Natural Areas Law of 1994.

Daw Khin Ma Ma Thwin

Educated at the Yangon University in nature sciences, Daw Khin Ma Ma Thwin started her career as an Environmental Education Officer.

She worked dedicatedly for the Division of Nature and Wildlife Conservation (NWCD) of the Forest Department, Ministry of Forestry for 18 years. During that time she conducted several special projects, including the Chatthin Community Education Project focused on the endemic Eld's Deer. As Myanmar representative she actively headed the data collection for the *Threatened Birds of Asia. The Birdlife International Red Data Book*. She also participated in the Waterfowl Census for Asian Wetland Bureau (now Wetlands International) for more than ten years. She was an instructor of Basic Wildlife Conservation Training for NWCD staff such as bird identification, and specimen preparation. She developed the environmental education program and also collected the bird specimens for Biodiversity Museum at Hlawga Wildlife Park where she served as curator.

She actively worked on the Baseline Study of Moyungyi Wetland Bird Sanctuary Project in 1998–1999 and an Inventory Project in early 2001 and late 2001 in collaboration with the Wild Bird Society of Japan.

U Aung Thant

After graduation from the State School of Fine Art, Yangon, where he studied from 1990 to 1994, U Aung Thant worked under such eminent artists as *Baggyi* (master) Aung Soe, U Ba Lone Lay and U Sonny Nyein. He later pursued a freelance career as an artist, and worked for Sarpay Beikhman and other leading publishers.

He spent nearly six months studying birds with U Kyaw Nyunt Lwin in various parts of the country before illustrating for this book.